Living with
Crack Cocaine

Living with Crack Cocaine

From a Husband's Regard

TOM MOUNT

authorHOUSE®

AuthorHouse™
1663 Liberty Drive
Bloomington, IN 47403
www.authorhouse.com
Phone: 1-800-839-8640

First published by AuthorHouse   09/27/2011

ISBN: 978-1-4567-6961-1 (sc)
ISBN: 978-1-4567-6963-5 (hc)
ISBN: 978-1-4567-6962-8 (ebk)

Library of Congress Control Number: 2011908022

Printed in the United States of America

Contents

INTRODUCTION ix

PREFACE xi

CHAPTER 1
Before Amy (BA) 1

CHAPTER 2
Then Came Amy 3

CHAPTER 3
Who Is Amy? 7

CHAPTER 4
What Is Cocaine and Crack Cocaine? 11

CHAPTER 5
Who Is a Crack Head? 17

CHAPTER 6
Magic in the Night... 19

CHAPTER 7
She's a People User 21

CHAPTER 8
My Name Is Crack 25

CHAPTER 9
Getting to Know Amy 29

CHAPTER 10
Too Many Back Alley Trips 33

CHAPTER 11
We Got Busted!... 37

CHAPTER 12
Am I an Enabler? / Tough Love.. 41

CHAPTER 13
Watch Your wallet 43

CHAPTER 14
Liar, Liar, Pants on Fire! 47

CHAPTER 15
Always Has Crack! 51

CHAPTER 16
Total Disregard for the Law.. 53

CHAPTER 17
Living by the Wrong Clock 55

CHAPTER 18
My Ignorance.. 57

CHAPTER 19
Crack Heads Are Irresponsible 61

CHAPTER 20
Always Second, Never First 65

CHAPTER 21
The Liability Is Yours 71

CHAPTER 22
Seek Professional Help! 73

CHAPTER 23
Codependency 77

CHAPTER 24
She Wants to Get Off of Crack! 83

CHAPTER 25
Disappearing Act 87

CHAPTER 26
Continually Left Alone 91

CHAPTER 27
Crack Addiction Help.. 95

CHAPTER 28
A Leopard Doesn't Change It's Spots! 97

CHAPTER 29
Tell Me Why.. 101

CHAPTER 30
Everything Comes to an End 103

CHAPTER 31
Recap 105

CHAPTER 32
    Some People Are Just Not Ready to Be Helped 107
APPENDIX A... 111
APPENDIX B 113
APPENDIX C 115
APPENDIX D... 117
ABOUT THE AUTHOR... 123
ABOUT THE BOOK.. 125

Introduction

Before I begin this book, I would like to introduce myself and tell you a few things about me.

My name is Tom Mount. I am retired and have never written a book before. After going through the usual retirement time wasters, I decided to try something new. Although this book is categorized as fiction (because I embellished a little bit to keep your interest up), the stories are true. I know because I lived through every one of them.

Amy (name changed) is a real person. She is my wife and, although she is addicted to crack cocaine, I love her with all my heart and soul. I have given up much to be with Amy. God only knows how long I will continue on with her before I can't take any more.

Thank you for purchasing my book. I hope you get as much out of reading it as I got out of writing it. Being the spouse of a person addicted to anything is not easy. Being the spouse of a person addicted to crack cocaine is one of the hardest things I have ever had to do.

I would like to say this, for the record:

I have never used crack cocaine, nor do I intend to ever use crack cocaine. My position is strictly as an outsider looking in on a spouse who is highly addicted. The purpose of this book is to show how the use of crack cocaine affects the spouse of the addicted person as well as the addict.

Tom Mount

Preface

This is the story of Amy Clemson. Amy is hopelessly addicted to crack cocaine. She has been using crack cocaine in excess of fifteen years. Although she would like to get off of the crack, Amy does not have the ability to do so. She cannot do it on her own, and she will not accept help. Unless Amy changes and accepts rehab, she may die a crack-related death.

Each chapter of this book will explore a different event in the path of Amy's life. We will attempt to look at what happened, why, and what could have been done differently. In the end, we will try to see what Amy can do to get off of the crack and live a normal life.

Amy should not be faulted for what she has done. She is under the control of crack cocaine. She does not always have control over the things she does. She is guided by crack. It is sad to see such a wonderful person keep going down further and further, to see her do things that she normally wouldn't do if she had control over her conscious mind. I hope and I pray that maybe someday, Amy will be able to kick her habit and see what a wonderful life is available to her without the use of drugs.

So, come along on a ride with Amy and me. We are happy to have you along. Just watch out for crack cocaine—he is out to get anyone he can to be his slave. Don't let him get you!

This book is mostly fiction; however, I tried my best to stick to the subject matter as related to crack cocaine abusers in general. The names of the players have been changed to protect me and them.

Chapter 1
Before Amy (BA)

I am going to start this book at six months BA (that's six months before I met Amy). That seems to be an appropriate amount of time for you to get to know me and be my friend. I own and operate a small business in the area. My hours are my own, so I get a little more free time than the average worker bee. I live alone, so there is no sense in going home to talk to the walls. My alternative has been to stop and have a beer or two at The Club.

The Club is a small neighborhood tavern located on the south side of Crackadelphia. Every day the same people visit The Club at the same time, sit in the same stools, drink the same drinks, and go home at the same time. There is more socialization than drinking at The Club, which is one of the few taverns I have ever been in that will allow you to stay and drink only soft drinks or coffee or water if you wish. Many of the older visitors drink nonalcoholic beer because they have been told not to drink alcohol by their doctors. It is a place to unwind from daily work activities before going home. There is a vast amount of knowledge to be found at The Club. The people who visit The Club range in age from around thirty to over eighty. There are people who have been visiting this place for over thirty-five years. The stories that are sometimes told about that building are amazing. It had been a stop on the railroad line from Crackadelphia to the New Jersey shore, and booze was sold out of the basement during prohibition. There is always some amount of conversation going on at the Club.

So that is where I went in the afternoons, before I went home. I used to tell everyone I only went to the Club on days that ended in "y." That would mean I would only go into the Club on Monday, Tuesday, Wednesday, Thursday, Friday, Saturday or Sunday. I have been keeping this schedule for around ten years. The afternoon crowd is friendly and around my age. We have things in common that we can talk about. I learned really quickly that if I need some work done at home, I can just put the word out at the Club, and someone will answer who can do that type of work. I have had lots of work done by people I know from the Club. I know they will do a good job because their reputation is on the line.

Occasionally, I will go to the Club in the evening. The Club has karaoke every night, and the place is full almost every evening. The crowd is much younger and more active. They are not there for conversation. They are there to sing karaoke and get drunk. It is interesting to go in there and listen to and watch these kids. And the psychedelic drinks they drink are beyond description. They are all designed for one purpose: to get you drunk—quick. The names of these drinks advertise their effects. There are drinks with names like Blow Job, Sex on the Beach, Come Screw Me Quickly, Mind Eraser, Jager Bomb, and many more I can't think of. The younger generation likes to mix energy drinks and alcohol for the effect. The energy drink is a stimulant, and the alcohol is a depressant. When you drink it, it acts upon the brain as a stimulant and a depressant at the same time. It really confuses the brain.

One evening, I wished there were some way to temporarily make a person invisible. I would hire a small school bus and pick up these kids' parents and bring them, invisible, to the Club. They would be amazed to see what their children do when they are out. I'll bet I could charge a good fare to have people spy on their kids. And I'll bet there would be some kids grounded after that.

Chapter 2

Then Came Amy

One evening, in September 2008, I went to the Club later than usual, just before nine. When I got there, the evening crowd was pretty much in place and waiting for karaoke to start. I looked around the bar and found one seat open. I sat there and ordered a beer. I greeted all the people I knew who were seated at the bar and started to settle in then looked around to see who was seated around me. Right next to me was an utterly beautiful young lady. Immediately I felt this charming lady was way out of my class. She was young, beautiful, and easy to talk to. Any man would crawl through fire and glass to get to her. Her hair was done perfectly, and her eyes kept saying, "Come to me." I was caught by her spell and stated to talk to her. Her name was Amy. Little did I know this would be the start of my adventures and misadventures with Amy. My whole life was about to change because of this one chance meeting. I spent the beginning of that evening talking to Amy, who was single and looking for fun. My kind of woman! She wasn't looking for any attachment, just fun.

I was having a great time with Amy. We laughed and drank and drank and laughed. Amy had this amazing little giggle that made you want to hear it over and over again. She was a perfect match for my personality. Where had she been all my life? I hoped the night would never end. I was sure she would be like Cinderella and disappear at the stroke of midnight. I was wrong—midnight came and went, and we were still there. We were still laughing and drinking and drinking and laughing. It was a great evening.

What came to an end? The bartender asked for last drink orders and yelled, "Last call for alcohol!" I was panic-stricken. Within minutes, I was going to lose my Cinderella. I had to think, and I had to think quickly. All night I had been trying to think of some way to keep her from leaving, but I was afraid if I came on too strong, I would never see her again. What to do, what to do. Finally it hit me. I remember her saying she had been dropped off by her daughter when she came to the Club. That would mean she needed a ride home. I got up the nerve and asked her, "Do you need a ride home?" She said yes, and I offered to take her to wherever she needed to go.

When we got into the car I asked her if she wanted to get something to eat. She said no. I decided to give it one last, game-winning shot. Why not go for broke? I leaned over, gave her a kiss, and asked her if she would like to go back to my place. To my surprise, she said yes. Now what was I going to do? I had this beautiful lady in my car, coming to my house, and I wasn't totally prepared. Little did I know this was the start of what was going to turn out to be a living hell for the next two years of my life.

So there I was. I had a very beautiful, very sexual lady in my car, and we were heading toward my house at three thirty in the morning. Various thoughts kept going through my head, but I knew I had to control myself. This was the equivalent of a first date. I didn't want to push too hard, but I wanted to let her know I was interested. The trip in the car to the house was rather quiet. I wish I could have read her mind. I know she was thinking about something. In many situations, women are not much different from men. They have needs and desires just like men do, except they are taught from the time they're little girls not to act on them. In our society, it is not acceptable for a woman to be the aggressor in a sexual encounter.

When we got to the house, we went inside and I put on some soft music. Luckily, I had a bottle of wine cooling in the refrigerator. I poured us each a glass and sat on the couch next to Amy. I was near enough to her to appear close, but not so near as to appear pushy.

We kept talking, and I learned some more things about Amy. Amy asked me if I had any drugs. I told her no, I didn't, and that I didn't do drugs. She appeared disappointed with that answer and told me she used crack cocaine occasionally. Crack cocaine meant nothing to me; I had never done any form of drugs in my life. One drug was the same as another to me. My drug education was about to begin under Professor Amy. The course of study was a two-year program, and the tuition was extremely high. I was not prepared for what I was about to get into.

As we sat on the couch, I kept moving closer and closer to Amy. She did not push me away or move away. When I got close enough, I put my arm around her and started kissing her. First the lips, then the ears, and then the neck. Amy returned the favor and gave a continual "Oh, yeah." More and more, we kept kissing rubbing, holding and seeking that elusive erogenous zone that would take us to complete sexual contentment. The passion kept getting higher and higher. I reached down and unbuttoned Amy's blouse and unhooked her bra. There, in the dim light, I could see Amy's perfect breasts standing straight out. I moved my head down and started kissing and sucking her nipples. They responded by becoming hard and standing straight out for me to nibble on them. Amy held my head in place and kept me doing what I had been doing. The soft "Oh yeah" coming from Amy had now graduated to a full yell. I could sense we had gone about as far as we could go on the couch. I moved up, kissed Amy on the ear, and whispered to her, "Would you like to go to the bedroom?" I asked. Amy responded with a kitten-like "Yes." I took her hand and led her down the hallway to what turned out to be a night I will always remember.

I remember one thing as being unusual with Amy. As soon as we each reached climax Amy immediately got up and out of bed and got dressed. No more holding, no more kissing, no more passion. It was over and Amy was ready to leave. As she was getting dressed Amy told me she was broke and needed money to buy food. She asked me if I would help her. I told her I would and she asked me for $60.00. I found out later that was the going price for a rock of crack cocaine. I got dressed and we left my house.

Let's look back at what I had just done. I let a complete stranger into my home in the middle of the night. Any number of things could have happened. She could have had a gun and caused me harm. She could have robbed me. She could have had an accomplice waiting for her and cleaned out my home. I was lucky none of this happened. In one short evening Amy now knew my vulnerable points and how to take advantage of them. She knew of all of my valuables and where they were in the house. She could come back when I wasn't home and clean me out. She had already told me she used crack cocaine. That meant she was a crack head, and I didn't pick up on it. Take a lesson from my stupidity and never do what I did. Amy had a drug addiction and needed money. She also knew she had an asset that only women have and knew how to use it. She knew how to make a man feel like King Kong and leave him wanting more. After only one night I was hooked by Amy's charms. I wanted to see more of her.

Chapter 3

Who Is Amy?

When the evening ended at my house, I asked Amy if I could take her home. Amy said yes but would not tell me where she lived. Instead of giving me an address, she gave me turn-by-turn directions to an apartment complex on the south side of Crackadelphia. She told me she lived with her grandparents. When we got to where we were going, Amy had me park by the rental office and got out of the car and disappeared in between the buildings. I am not used to that type of exit. I try to be a gentleman when I take a lady out and at least walk her to the door when I bring her home. Amy would have no part of it. She wanted to keep her address and living arrangements confidential. At first I was confused by this, but as you will see, I soon figured out why she did it this way.

Before she got out of the car, I made arrangements to see her again the next evening. This time she gave me an address where to pick her up.

At the predetermined time, I went to meet Amy at 123 Normal Street. I pulled up in front of the house and, as requested, turned off my headlights and waited. It wasn't very long until a young girl came out from the house. She walked up to the car and said, "Hi, are you waiting for Amy?" She was young (probably around twenty-five years old at the most) and was wearing a short halter top and a very short skirt. It was obvious by the way she was dressed what she was looking for.

I replied, "Yes, I am. Why do you ask?"

She said, "Because we both do the same thing, and I am better." She pulled up her skirt and exposed her genitals. She was wearing no undergarments and obviously was ready for action. She had two piercings on her labia and a design shaved into her pubic hair. "Would you like some of this right now?" she asked.

I was dumbfounded. I had no answer to give her. I told her, "No, I think I will wait for Amy." She asked to get into the car with me, and I told her no.

She said, "What's the difference? We both work out of the same house."

Then it hit me—was Amy a prostitute? I didn't know anything about her. I had just met her. Maybe this explains why she had been so good in bed the night before. I sat and I waited. I waited about forty-five minutes before Amy finally came out. When I told her what had happened, she got all upset. She said this girl does that all the time, and it wasn't true. We went to the Club and had a few drinks.

The evening was just a few drinks and small talk. Amy was not much of a talker. One thing I noticed about Amy was that she did not like to talk about herself and kept many things to herself. She was almost secretive about herself and her past. You will see later, in this book, why.

After we had been at the Club for about an hour, Amy asked me if I would take her to get something from a friend. When we got into the car, Amy would not tell me where we were going but rather gave me turn-here directions. We drove around the near east side of Crackadelphia for about an hour. Amy kept giving me directions. It seemed like we were going noplace. I noticed we crossed the same streets several times. Finally Amy said, "Pull over here, and turn your lights off." Amy got out of the car and disappeared down the street. I could not see where she went. I was nervous about what I was doing. Amy had me parked in a dark part of the street, in an area I was not familiar with. I waited and waited, and Amy did not return.

Finally, after two hours of waiting, I called the phone number Amy had given me. The number was to her mother's house, and her brother answered the phone. I told him what had happened and that I was worried about her safety. He said she was probably inside smoking crack. He said if I would pick him up and take him there, he would go inside and tell her to come out. I did as he asked and brought him back to the house where I thought Amy was. I parked in the same spot, and he got out of the car. I sat and waited for over an hour. Finally, I had had my fill, and I left. Amy and her brother were both still inside that house. That was my first experience with crack cocaine. It makes people very rude and uncaring.

Now I'll address the issue of why Amy had me pick her up and drop her off at the rental office and then disappear between the buildings. Remember how she had told me she was staying with her grandparents? Well, I found out that was a lie.

One afternoon, when I was supposed to pick up Amy, I got there a little early. I walked between the buildings that Amy most frequently used and hid in the bushes. From my vantage point I could see which apartment Amy would come out of and still get back to the car before she did. I now knew which apartment Amy was staying in. I took my newly found information and went back to the car to wait for Amy.

The next day, when I was sure Amy wasn't home, I went back to the apartment. I knocked on the door and waited to see who answered the knock. Before too long a Hispanic gentleman came to the door. I introduced myself and showed him a picture of Amy. I asked him if he knew her. He said, "That is my roommate's girlfriend." I thanked him and left. I had just found out Amy had a boyfriend and was living with him.* Apparently, he was quite liberal and never questioned where Amy was and what she had been doing when she didn't come home for days or weeks at a time. Long term absences were not unusual for Amy. When she was on a binge she could be gone for as long as two weeks with no explanation upon her return.

*I shouldn't speculate as to what her living conditions were. I had just met her, I didn't own her.

Chapter 4

What Is Cocaine and Crack Cocaine?

Reprinted by permission
from the National Institute on Drug Abuse

How Is Cocaine Abused?

Cocaine is a powerfully addictive stimulant drug. The powdered hydrochloride salt form of cocaine can be snorted or dissolved in water and then injected. Crack is the street name given to the form of cocaine that has been processed to make a rock crystal, which, when heated, produces vapors that are smoked. The term "crack" refers to the crackling sound produced by the rock as it is heated.

Three routes of administration are commonly used for cocaine: snorting, injecting, and smoking. Snorting is the process of inhaling cocaine powder through the nose, where it is absorbed into the bloodstream through the nasal tissues. Injecting is the use of a needle to insert the drug directly into the bloodstream. Smoking involves inhaling cocaine vapor or smoke into the lungs, where absorption into the bloodstream is as rapid as it is by injection. All three methods of cocaine abuse can lead to addiction and other severe health problems, including increasing the risk of contracting HIV/AIDS and other infectious diseases.

The intensity and duration of cocaine's effects—which include increased energy, reduced fatigue, and mental alertness—depend on the route of drug administration. The faster cocaine is absorbed into the bloodstream and delivered to the brain, the more intense the high. Injecting or smoking cocaine produces a quicker, stronger high than snorting. On the other hand, faster absorption usually means shorter duration of action: the high from snorting cocaine may last 15 to 30 minutes, but the high from smoking may last only 5 to 10 minutes. In order to sustain the high, a cocaine abuser has to administer the drug again. For this reason, cocaine is sometimes abused in binges—taken repeatedly within a relatively short period of time, at increasingly higher doses.

How Does Cocaine Affect the Brain?

Cocaine is a strong central nervous system stimulant that increases levels of dopamine, a brain chemical (or neurotransmitter) associated with pleasure and movement, in the brain's reward circuit. Certain brain cells, or neurons, use dopamine to communicate. Normally, dopamine is released by a neuron in response to a pleasurable signal (e.g., the smell of good food), and then recycled back into the cell that released it, thus shutting off the signal between neurons. Cocaine acts by preventing the dopamine from being recycled, causing excessive amounts of the neurotransmitter to build up, amplifying the message to and response of the receiving neuron, and ultimately disrupting normal communication. It is this excess of dopamine that is responsible for cocaine's euphoric effects. With repeated use, cocaine can cause long-term changes in the brain's reward system and in other brain systems as well, which may eventually lead to addiction. With repeated use, tolerance to the cocaine high also often develops. Many cocaine abusers report that they seek but fail to achieve as much pleasure as they did from their first exposure. Some users will increase their dose in an attempt to intensify and prolong the euphoria, but this can also increase the risk of adverse psychological or physiological effects.

What Adverse Effects Does Cocaine Have on Health?

Abusing cocaine has a variety of adverse effects on the body. For example, cocaine constricts blood vessels, dilates pupils, and increases body temperature, heart rate, and blood pressure. It can also cause headaches and gastrointestinal complications such as abdominal pain and nausea. Because cocaine tends to decrease appetite, chronic users can become malnourished as well.

Different methods of taking cocaine can produce different adverse effects. Regular intranasal use (snorting) of cocaine, for example, can lead to loss of the sense of smell; nosebleeds; problems with swallowing; hoarseness; and a chronically runny nose. Ingesting cocaine can cause severe bowel gangrene as a result of reduced blood flow. Injecting cocaine can bring about severe allergic reactions and increased risk for contracting HIV/AIDS and other blood-borne diseases. Binge-patterned cocaine use may lead to irritability, restlessness, and anxiety. Cocaine abusers can also experience severe paranoia—a temporary state of full-blown paranoid psychosis—in which they lose touch with reality and experience auditory hallucinations.

Regardless of the route or frequency of use, cocaine abusers can experience acute cardiovascular or cerebrovascular emergencies, such as a heart attack or stroke, which may cause sudden death. Cocaine-related deaths are often a result of cardiac arrest or seizure followed by respiratory arrest.

Added Danger: Coca ethylene

Polydrug use—use of more than one drug—is common among substance abusers. When people consume two or more psychoactive drugs together, such as cocaine and alcohol, they compound the danger each drug poses and unknowingly perform a complex chemical experiment within their bodies. Researchers have found that the human liver combines cocaine and alcohol to produce a third substance, coca ethylene, which intensifies cocaine's euphoric effects. Coca ethylene is associated with a greater risk of sudden death than cocaine alone.

What Treatment Options Exist?

Behavioral interventions—particularly, cognitive-behavioral therapy—have been shown to be effective for decreasing cocaine use and preventing relapse. Treatment must be tailored to the individual patient's needs in order to optimize outcomes—this often involves a combination of treatment, social supports, and other services.

Currently, there are no FDA-approved medications for treating cocaine addiction; thus, developing a medication to treat cocaine and other forms of addiction remains one of NIDA's top research priorities. Researchers are seeking to develop medications that help alleviate the severe craving associated with cocaine addiction, as well as medications that counteract cocaine-related relapse triggers, such as stress. Several compounds are currently being investigated for their safety and efficacy, including a vaccine that would sequester cocaine in the bloodstream and prevent it from reaching the brain. Current research suggests that while medications are effective in treating addiction, combining them with a comprehensive behavioral therapy program is the most effective method to reduce drug use in the long term.

How Widespread Is Cocaine Abuse?

Monitoring the Future Survey*

According to the 2009 Monitoring the Future survey—a national survey of 8th-, 10th-, and 12th-graders—there were continuing declines reported in the use of powder cocaine, with past-year†† usage levels reaching their lowest point since the early 1990s. Significant declines in use were measured from 2008 to 2009 among 12th-graders across all three survey categories: lifetime use decreased from 7.2 percent to 6.0 percent; past-year use dropped from 4.4 percent to 3.4 percent; and past-month use dropped from 1.9 percent to 1.3 percent. Survey measures showed other positive findings among 12th-graders as well; their perceived risk of harm associated with powder cocaine use increased significantly during the same period. Additionally, survey participants in the 10th grade reported significant changes, with past-month use falling from 1.2 percent in 2008 to 0.9 percent in 2009.

Use of Cocaine by Students 2008
Monitoring the Future Survey

	8th-Graders	10th-Graders	12th-Graders
Lifetime**	2.6%	4.6%	6.0%
Past Year	1.6	2.7	34
Past Month	0.8	0.9	1.3

Crack Cocaine Use by Students
2009 Monitoring the Future Survey

	8th-Graders	10th-Graders	12th-Graders
Lifetime**	1.7%	2.1%	2.4%
Past Year	1.1	1.2	1.3
Past Month	0.5	0.4	0.6

National Survey on Drug Use and Health (NSDUH)***

According to the 2008 National Survey on Drug Use and Health, the estimated percentage of persons aged 12 or older who used cocaine in the past month (0.7 percent) was similar to the percentage in 2007 and 2002. However, the percentage of past-month crack users in 2008 (0.1 percent of the population) was lower than in 2007 and all other years going back to 2002, with the exception of 2004. From 2002 to 2008, rates of past-month cocaine use among youth aged 12 to 17 declined significantly, from 0.6 percent to 0.4 percent. Past-month cocaine use also dropped significantly among young adults aged 18 to 25 during this time period, from 2.0 percent to 1.5 percent.

Significant declines in the number or percentage of past-year cocaine initiates were also estimated among several age groups measured, including persons 12 or older and those aged 18 to 25. The percentage of past-year initiates also dropped significantly from 2007 to 2008 for crack use among the 12-17 age groups.

Other Information Sources

For additional information on cocaine, please refer to the following sources on NIDA's Web site, www.drugabuse.gov:

- Research Report: Cocaine Abuse and Addiction
- NIDA Notes: Articles on Cocaine

For a list of street terms used to refer to cocaine and other drugs, visit www.whitehousedrugpolicy.gov/streetterms/default.asp.

1 Harris DS, et al. The pharmacology of coca ethylene in humans following cocaine and ethanol administration. Drug Alcohol Depend 72(2):169-182, 2003.

* These data are from the 2009 Monitoring the Future survey, funded by the National Institute on Drug Abuse, National Institutes of Health, Department of Health and Human Services, and conducted annually by the University of Michigan's Institute for Social Research. The survey has tracked 12th-graders' illicit drug use and related attitudes since 1975; in 1991, 8th—and 10th-graders were added to the study. The latest data are online at www.drugabuse.gov.

** "Lifetime" refers to use at least once during a respondent's lifetime. "Past year" refers to use at least once during the year preceding an individual's response to the survey. "Past month" refers to use at least once during the 30 days preceding an individual's response to the survey.

*** NSDUH (formerly known as the National Household Survey on Drug Abuse) is an annual survey of Americans aged 12 and older conducted by the Substance Abuse and Mental Health Services Administration. This survey is available online at www.samhsa.gov and from NIDA at 877-643-2644.

Revised 3/10

Chapter 5

Who Is a Crack Head?

People of any race can live to hit that nasty-ass rock. They're usually very thin and dirty, and they smell like warm trash, spoiled milk, fecal matter, rotting corpses, etc. They frequently bob, weave, and twitch, and they have periodic spurts of high energy. They've always got something for sale or know somebody that has just what you need. The most severe crack heads can be viewed in the wild missing standard items like shoes, socks, <u>and teeth</u>. If you come into contact with a crack head, it is suggested that you secure all valuables and avoid any physical contact or direct contact with their breath (could cause dizziness and/or vomiting). If you lose property to a crack head, accept the loss. If you find yourself chasing a crack head, accept the loss—crack heads are fast, they be gettin' somewhere. You ain't catching no crack head. That guy couldn't stay still for a second. That guy radiated a heavy fecal smell.

Some guy took my quarter from the payphone, and I chased him. Damn, that guy was fast for a homeless-lookin' fecal smeller.

Amy is not quite that bad (yet), but she is well on her way. She lives out of the trunk of her car and sleeps in the back seat. She is homeless by any definition. Amy bathes only when the opportunity presents itself, which is once every three or four days. Her main goal in life is to secure the next hit of crack cocaine.

I took Amy off of the street and tried to change her into a normal person. I have a codependent personality trait. In my mind, I am here to help and change everyone. I seek out people who I think need me, and I try to change them. I will say that this seldom works. People do not change.

Some More Personal Experiences

If a person constantly asks you for money in exchange for their car, he or she is probably a crack head. Amy rents her car to the crack dealers in exchange for a piece of a rock. Both parties are satisfied with the deal. If the dealer gets busted, it will be Amy's car that will be seized.

If a person is in the bathroom for over an hour, has the bathroom fan on, turns the shower on, but comes out an hour later not wet, that person is most likely a crack head—or up to something.

If a person says he or she is going to the drug store for one thing and doesn't come back, that person is probably on a crack binge. Amy has done this to me many times. She knows I probably won't follow her, because deep down inside, I want to trust her and believe in her.
MacMillian Dictionary defines crack head as someone who uses the illegal drug crack a lot.

Crack heads are stereotyped people. They have come to be known as liars, cheats, and thieves. They are people who are not to be trusted in your home alone. If you know a crack head will be in your home, you should take inventory of all of your valuables and put them in a safe place. This does not mean that any person who has smoked crack cocaine once is a crack head; this is not true. There are some really good recovering crack heads out there. Seek them out, they can help you.

Chapter 6

Magic in the Night

Amy and I were getting along pretty well. Our relationship was progressing smoothly. We had a unique relationship in the beginning. We each had a need to be satisfied and we each had the ability to do that for the other. I had a very high sexual appetite and Amy was addicted to crack cocaine and needed money to buy it.

We each satisfied each other's needs without any qualms. That was until Amy got greedy and decided to push our agreement to the next level.

As time went on Amy and I started spending more and more time together. She finally left her boyfriend and moved in with me. All was going well and we were both happy with our relationship. We had been together for about four months when I started noticing I had less money in my pocket when I woke up than was there when I went to bed. I always questioned Amy about it and she always denied knowing anything about it. She always said I must have spent it and didn't remember it. I could see that as a possibility once or twice, over a period of time, but this was happening much too often. This must be magic; things keep disappearing when I go to sleep. Maybe I need to call Sherlock Holmes. I finally took to sleeping with my money and my wallet under the mattress on my side of the bed. I did that until I had a wall safe installed in the bedroom. Today, I keep my valuables locked up when I go to bed. After all, remember, Amy is a crack head.

This one is really going to get you. One night, Amy and I went to bed as usual and went to sleep. For some reason I woke up around 3:00 a.m. I rolled over and noticed Amy was in bed next to me and sound asleep. Not wanting to disturb her I tried to go back to sleep. After about thirty minutes of trying to sleep, I resigned myself to the fact that I wasn't going to go back to sleep. I decided to roll over the other way and snuggle Amy. Maybe that would help me sleep. I put my arm around her and low and behold, *alakazam*, she wasn't there. It was a pillow under the blankets. I got right up, out of bed. I searched the whole house looking for Amy. Not only wasn't Amy there but my money and car were gone also. She got me! I started trying to call her on her cell phone, but she wouldn't answer. She knew she did me wrong and she knew I would be angry.

So now what do I do? I have no car and I have no money. It's 4:00 a.m. and I am stuck. I have to go to work in four hours and I don't know how I am going to get there. I will have to call my son to come and get me. Amy was not thinking about me or what she had done to me; she was only thinking about getting a hit off of that rock. What a sad life she had. She was allowing her life to be dictated to by a piece of dope. I wished I could help her but couldn't. She didn't want help; she only wanted crack.

Chapter 7

She's a People User

Don't forget who you are dealing with: she is a crack head and a people user. No matter what she says, you are only there for one reason: so she can get crack. You may or may not be in the picture if she were not a crack head. Maybe she loves you, maybe she doesn't, and it's immaterial. What she cares about is that you have enough money so she can get crack.

Be careful. As a people user, she will have a contingency plan in effect. She will have someone else or some other way of getting money waiting in the wings should anything happen to your relationship. Remember, this is not about love or feelings; it's about being able to continue on with her crack habit.

I like to compare crack heads to Pony Express riders. They would get on a horse and ride it as far and as fast as they could. When the horse was ready to die, they would dump that horse and find a new one. Then they would start the process all over with the new horse. Their goal was to get from point A to point B as fast as possible, with the least amount of hassle. Being a crack head is similar. You find someone to support you with the idea of a long-range future, and then you use his money and assets as fast as possible. When he can no longer support you, you dump him and find a new person to start the process all over again. A crack head may use more than one man at a time. She may split between the two of them and get money from both of them. Of course there must be some form of repayment for the money; usually it is sex.

Crack heads must do this if they are going to continue using crack. Although the trend of crack prices is down since 1986, it is still expensive in relation to other drugs (see Appendix C). Most crack heads cannot

Tom Mount

afford to continue using crack cocaine without some sort of financial assistance, be it legal or illegal.

Crack heads must be resourceful in their choice of a source of money (their money train). The use and possession of crack cocaine is still illegal in most parts of the world and so is giving financial help to purchase it. The money train must either accept the risk of getting caught or not know where his money is going. Most nonusers will probably opt out of any financial help for an illegal activity; therefore, the crack head will lie about where the money is going. The crack head may ask for rent money, gas money, food money, utility bill money, or any combination or variation of any of the above.

If crack heads find a large source of money, it is safe to say they will hang on to that source for as long as possible. But watch out—they will cheat and steal at the same time. Nothing is safe from a crack head. When I met Amy, I had a fairly well decorated home. Today, most or the walls are barren. Knickknacks are gone. My collectables are all gone. I have little left of my former life. Amy has taken all of it and either pawned it or sold it. Nothing is safe. If I want to keep anything, I have to get it out of this house.

When we got married, I bought Amy a very nice and fairly expensive wedding ring set. I did as much as I could, with the idea that these rings would last her a lifetime. They lasted two weeks. She pawned them. She used the money to buy her crack. When I found out, I went to the pawn shop and bought them back. I gave the rings back to her and made her promise she would not pawn them again. Well, she kept her word and did not pawn them. She sold them to the crack dealer, and he sold them to a pawn shop. We never saw those rings again. All told, in the two years we have been married, I have bought Amy four sets of wedding rings, counting the times I bought them back from the pawn shop. I don't know why I did that; I just wanted to make sure she had a ring on her finger so everyone knew she was married.

Remember this! Never buy crack heads jewelry or anything else that can be pawned or sold. They invariably run out of money before they run out of the need for crack. They know where every pawn shop is and will pawn or sell everything they have for one more hit.

Always remember that crack heads will lie, cheat, steal, or do almost anything else to get the money they need for their crack. If you come between crack heads and their ability to get crack, you will be sacrificed. Do not trust them or believe anything they say. They are using you to get what they want—crack.

Keep in mind the reverse is also true. If you are looking for a deal on jewelry or any other small item, find a crack head who needs money. Crack heads will sell almost anything they have really cheap. Just beware—you never know where they got what they are selling. It may be stolen, and that could be a problem for you.

Chapter 8

My Name Is Crack

Before I get too far into this book, I want to share a poem I found on the Internet. Every time I read it, it sends a chill up my spine and asks the question, "Why would anyone use Crack Cocaine?"

My Name Is Crack
by Anonymous

My name is Crack
I destroy homes . . . I tear families apart.

I take your children . . . and that's just the <u>start</u>.

I'm more costly than diamonds, more precious than gold.

The sorrow I bring is a sight to behold.

If you need me, remember, I'm easily found . . .

I live all around you . . . in <u>schools</u> and in town.

I live with the rich . . . I live with the poor . . .

I live down the street . . . maybe even next door!

I am made in such ways . . . you can shoot me or smoke . . .

I used to be called "cocaine" . . . or "coke."

The sound that I make when you're inhaling my stench . . .

Is how my name Crack came to be . . . (perfect sense).

My power is awesome; try me, you'll see . . .

But if you do, you may never break free.

Just try me once, and I may let you go . . .

But try me twice, and I'll own your soul.

When I possess you, you'll steal and you'll lie.

You'll do what you have to, just to get high.

The crimes you'll commit, for my narcotic charms . . .

Will be worth the pleasure you'll feel in your arms, lungs, and nose.

You'll lie to your mother; you'll steal from your dad. . . .

When you see their tears, you should feel sad.

But you will forget your morals . . . and how you were raised?

I'll be your conscience . . . I'll teach you my ways.

I'll take kids from parents, and parents from kids.

I turn people from God . . . . and <u>separate</u> friends.

I'll take everything from you, your looks and your pride.

I'll be with you ALWAYS . . . right by your side.

You'll give up everything . . . your family; your home. . . .

Your friends, your money . . . then you'll be all alone.

I'll take and take; till you have nothing more to give . . .

When I'm finished with you . . . you'll be lucky to live.

If you try me, be warned . . . this is no game . . .

If given the chance . . . I'll drive you insane!

I'll ravish your body . . . I'll control your mind . . .

I'll own you completely . . . your soul will be mine!

The nightmares I'll give you, while lying in bed . . .

The voices you'll hear . . . from inside your head . . .

The sweats, the shakes . . . the visions you'll see . . .

I want you to know . . . these are *all* gifts from me.

But then it's too late, and you'll know in your heart . . .

That you are *mine* . . . and we shall not part . . .

You'll regret that you tried me . . . they always do . . .

But *you* came to *me* . . . Not I to you . . .

You knew this would happen . . . many times you were told . . .

But you challenged my power . . . and chose to be bold.

You could have said no . . . and just walked away . . .

If you could live that day over . . . now what would you say?

I'll be your master . . . and you'll be my slave . . .

I'll even go with you . . . when you go to your grave.

Now that you have met me . . . what will you do?

Will you try me or not? It's all up to you. . . .

I can bring you more misery than words can tell . . .

Come take my hand . . . let me lead you to Hell!

Chapter 9

Getting to Know Amy

Getting to know Amy is not an easy thing to do. She has a wall built around her and will not allow anyone in. She will never divulge or discuss anything about her past. She is a very secretive person. After almost two years, I know little about Amy.

Amy is a very rebellious person. She is obviously fighting the system in every direction. At times Amy will go out of her way to break the law and then defy the police to come after her. When she is in her environment, she is like an alley cat. She knows the back streets and alleys better than most people. With a two-minute head start, Amy can disappear for days.

Amy is a cute-looking person. She will stop conversations when she enters a room. If she is given the opportunity to have the proper wardrobe, she can be said to be very attractive. She is five feet, two inches, and has brown hair and green eyes. She has extra-wide hips and has trouble keeping her weight down. Amy loves to eat and sleep. Her appetite will match that of an over-the-road trucker.

When you get to know Amy, it is obvious that she has a mental handicap. She appears to have the mental maturity of about a sixteen-year-old child, which explains why she gets along so well with children. Her educational level is sixth grade, which was the last full year she attended school successfully. That does not mean Amy is not intelligent. Amy is very intelligent; she just hasn't had the education to help her capitalize on her intelligence.

Amy has had four children, all of which she gave up at or shortly after birth. She has no regular contact with her children. She sees them occasionally, when it fits into her schedule. Her oldest daughter has given

Amy two grandchildren, who she sees occasionally. Amy's tolerance level with children is about thirty minutes.

In speaking with her family members and the father of two of her children, I found out Amy never stopped smoking crack—even when she was pregnant with two of her children. I am told that immediately after she gave birth to one of her children, her sister brought a piece of a rock to the hospital and Amy smoked it in the bathroom. When she came home from the hospital with that child, she stayed home with the child for two hours and then left and did not return for two days. She was obviously binging on crack cocaine. This should tell you just how far a crack head will go for that next hit. Nothing takes precedence over crack to a crack head. Even the mother instinct will not supersede the urge and need for crack.

Amy has no skills with which to get a job. She worked for me in the shipping business for a short time, and it was obvious her attention span is very short. Again, she would defy authority at every opportunity.

Amy is a very sexual person. This would explain her ability to get and trap men for her own using. She is not afraid to use her femininity to get what she wants. Although she has all the tools, it is obvious Amy does not like men. She uses men because she has to in order to survive, but she does not really like them. This is obvious in that Amy likes masturbation and self-stimulation over intercourse. On the nonsexual side, Amy enjoys the company of women over men. Amy claims to be bisexual.

Amy is a perpetual liar, cheat, and a thief. She fits the crack addict mold perfectly. She is a convicted felon and has been in prison several times. Amy thrives in prison. She has been called "Smiley" while in prison because she always has a smile on her face. My visits to her in prison have always been enjoyable, and Amy has never expressed a disliking of the prison system. She follows direction well and does not cause any trouble. She is a model offender.

Amy is not an easy person to get along with. She is a loner rather than a team player. If crossed, Amy can be a very dangerous person. She will fight over the littlest things. She has no fear of authority and will defy the rules for no reason.

If Amy is caught in a lie, she will not back down. She will fabricate her story and stick to it no matter what. The more I argue with her, the deeper she digs in. It's almost like she brings herself to believe what she is saying.

It is very hard to describe Amy, because she changes so often and so drastically. She can be your best friend and lover at one moment and then change and be your worst enemy the next. She can adapt to any situation and bend it to make it to her liking. Amy is not trustworthy. When Amy is in your home, you have to watch everything she does or she will steal anything you have. She has nothing that belongs to her; she has stolen everything that she has.

If you get involved with an Amy-type person, be careful; they can be your worst nightmare. Amy was mine.

Chapter 10

Too Many Back Alley Trips

It was Friday night, and I didn't have to work the next day. I could stay up late and it wouldn't interfere with my job. Amy was supposed to come over. She has a bad habit of being late or not showing up at all. I was not going to wait all night for her. It was seven; if Amy was not there by ten, I would leave. I didn't care if I saw her or not. Except for the sex, we really didn't have anything in common, and she wasn't much fun. All Amy ever wanted to do was get drunk or get high. So if she didn't show up, that would be okay. I could have more fun by myself. Maybe I could even find somebody who wanted to be nice to me.

At nine thirty, Amy finally showed up. I didn't know what took her so long, but at least she was there. This was typical behavior for Amy. We sat in the living room and had small talk conversation. Neither one of us had much to say. We talked for about twenty minutes, and then I was tired of saying nothing. I got up and started doing things around the house. Amy sat on the couch and watched TV. This, too, was pretty boring.

About eleven thirty, Amy came up to me and said, "Take me for a ride."

I asked her, "Where are we going?" I knew where we were going I just wanted to hear her say it.

Amy replied, "You know." As soon as we got into the car, Amy turned to me and said, "Give me sixty dollars."

At first I said no, but I knew she would insist and keep on until she got the money. I didn't want to go through that, so I gave her the money. We took off driving. As usual it was "turn here, turn there" directions. She didn't want me to know where we were going, and when we got there she didn't want me to know where we were. She was acting like this was a secret CIA mission and she was their top agent. We were just going on a drug run. People do it all the time.

When we finally got to where we were going, Amy told me to stop and turn off the lights. We were in a very dark alley behind some really run-down houses. Amy got out of the car and started walking down the alley. I couldn't see very much, but I could see enough to know she met with someone a little way down the alley. They talked for a few minutes, and then Amy came back to the car. She gave me the same "turn here" directions to get me back to where I knew where I was.

It's funny to hear her make her buy. She calls a number, and when they answer, she says, "This is Amy, sixty, I'm pullin' up." If that sounds like some kind of code, that's because it is. I call it Crack Talk. This is what she just said: "This is Amy." The drug dealers know their customers and their drugs of choice; nothing else need be said. The dealer knows this is a buy of crack cocaine. "Sixty" simply means she has $60 cash with which to buy the drug. "I'm pullin' up" means Amy is in the neighborhood and is ready to make a buy. So from that simple sentence, the drug dealer knows who is buying, what is being sold, and when this buy will go down.

When Amy got back into the car, she couldn't wait to get a hit off of her new purchase. She slid down in the seat and pulled out her crack pipe and got a quick hit. I don't like her doing that. If we got pulled over, I would then be involved.

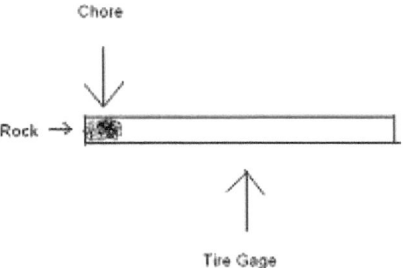

Typical Crack Pipe

When we got back to the house, Amy immediately went to the bathroom and locked the door. She would be in there for fifteen to thirty minutes. That was where she liked to do her thing with the crack, and she didn't like to be watched. When she was done using, she would open the door and come out of the bathroom. Her eyes would be dilated, her speech would be slowed, and she would be totally paranoid and hear and see things that are not there. This is what is called "tweaking." She would then start to tear the house apart while looking for a piece of the crack rock that she thought she might have dropped. She would dump out and look in trash cans, remove heat vents, look in the duct work, and tear up carpet and look underneath. When she was done, the house would be a mess; and she would not have found anything. She would not remember doing any of this, and she would not admit to doing any of it. Amy could be dangerous during this time. She would have newfound strength, and she would use it if cornered. She was looking for crack that she thought she had dropped or lost. If she became convinced you had it, she would fight you for it. It was best to just stay in the background and only jump in if she was about to destroy something valuable or hurt herself or someone else. This whole process takes from one and a half to two hours.

Okay, so there you have it, a drug deal and usage from beginning to end. Seems pretty simple. But the night wasn't over. That was just the first trip. After three in the morning, Amy was coming down off of her last high. She came to me. "I need sixty dollars," she said. "And I need a ride." I knew what this meant. Amy wanted, or needed, more crack. At first I tried to say no, but I had to be careful. Amy was going to get her crack one way or another. She was capable of almost anything when she was put in this position. She would lie, cheat, steal, or turn to prostitution to get the money for the crack. Once, I had told her no and stuck to it. She took off and went on a binge. I didn't see her for a week. I didn't want that to happen again. I didn't have much choice; I had to give in.

So off we went to visit the crack man. I was given the same "turn here" directions. We may or may not have been going to the same place. Amy knew many places to get what she wanted.

That's three trips in one night. That's $180 spent on crack in one night. If she averaged six nights a week, that's $1,080 a week, or $56,160 a year. Is there any wonder why crack-addicted people are like they are and do what they do? A crack cocaine addiction is expensive! Most crack heads do not use every day; they use crack when they can and supplement with other drugs when they cannot use crack.

Chapter 11

We Got Busted!

It was a rather warm September night, and I was supposed to see Amy. We had been seeing each other for about three weeks, and things seemed to be going pretty well. We seemed to have a good time whenever we were together. I was starting to feel really comfortable with Amy.

Amy did not have a car, so I always had to meet her somewhere. She never let me pick her up at her apartment. She was someplace different every time and had to tell me how to get there. This night she asked me to meet her at the Fast Times Bar. This was one of the places were Amy hung out. It was kind of a rough-looking place, the kind of a place where you want somebody to watch your back. Keep you money in your pocket and watch what you say to whom. But this is where Amy hung out, and these were her people.

We had a couple of beers, and Amy asked if we could go to my house and listen to music. Of course I said yes—I still had memories of that first night I took her there. We finished our drinks and left the Fast Times Bar. I was glad to be out of there.

Since the weather was so nice, I had decided to drive my BMW Z4 Roadster that night. It was a sharp car, and Amy had never seen it. I wanted to impress her, and I wanted all of her friends to see her in it with me. I did both very well.

When we got to the car, Amy asked if we could stop someplace so she could pick something up. I didn't see any harm, so I said okay. Amy gave me her usual "turn here" directions, and pretty soon we were on a very dark back street in a rundown neighborhood. Amy asked me to pull over, turn off my lights, and wait. Amy got out and disappeared down a dark alley. After about fifteen minutes, Amy returned, got in the car and said, "Let's go to your place." I was glad to get moving and get out of that neighborhood.

We hadn't gone very far before the red lights and spotlight came on behind us. I wondered what I had done. The BMW is a pretty fast car, so I thought maybe I had been speeding and didn't know it. Amy turned to me and told me not to say anything; she would take care of it. I noticed she was putting something behind her back. Two police officers came up to the car, one on each side. I could tell they seemed to know Amy. They called her by name before they asked for any ID. They had us both get out of the car, and they patted me down. They took us each in different directions, one in front of the car and one behind it. The officer questioned me as to where we had been and what we were doing. He told me the house where she went was a crack house, and they had it staked out. He asked me, "Do you know her very well?" I said, "No, I just met her three weeks ago." He told me who she was and told me she was a drug addict. He told me I was the seventh older gentleman that she had been stopped with this week. He said that was how she got her drug money. She made men like me feel good and then got money from us. I really felt stupid, but she already had me hooked with her feminine charms. Being the codependent person that I am, I instantly thought that she needed me and that I could change her into what I was looking for. That made her even more attractive to me.

The officer finished questioning me and then had me go sit on the front steps of a nearby vacant house. He told me they knew I hadn't done anything wrong; they were looking for Amy. He asked me if they could search my car. I said yes and gave him the keys. Both police officers searched my car. I looked over at Amy. She was handcuffed with her hands behind her back. Her back was toward me. I watched her as she stuck her finger into her waistband and flipped something out onto the ground.

When they finished searching the car, they went back over to Amy and started talking to her. While they were searching the car, they searched her purse and found her crack pipe and other drug paraphernalia. While they were talking to her, they shined the light on the ground around her. They found what she had flipped from her waistband: a rock of crack cocaine. They asked her if it was hers, and she said no. They told her they had found her crack pipe and if she admitted to the crack being hers, they would give her a ticket for possession of drug paraphernalia and let it go at that. If she wouldn't admit to it, they would arrest her and take her to jail for the night and let her see the judge in the morning. Amy admitted the crack was hers, and they gave her a ticket. The police told us to leave the area, and we all got in our cars and left.

As soon as we pulled away, Amy started giving me her "turn here" directions. I told her I know how to get to my house. She said, "No, we have to make a stop first." I couldn't believe it—she was taking me to another crack house. She had me park in a dark alley with my lights out. I wasn't parked there five minutes when those same two police officers pulled up behind me. Again, they told me to leave the area. This time they followed me to make sure I did it. I went straight home and did not look back. I didn't know how Amy got home that night, and I really didn't care.

Chapter 12

Am I an Enabler? / Tough Love

What Is an Enabler?

An enabler is someone who, despite knowing that a behavior is destructive or harmful, allows a loved one to continue to do it. It is frequently used in context of addiction. For example, a crack cocaine addict may have an enabler friend who still encourages him to go to a crack house just for one hit.

Most enablers feel that they are actually helping or supporting the addict. They think that they're protecting him or understanding him, or just helping the person have a little fun.

In this fashion, though the enabler may be acting out of love and trying to help or protect a person, he or she is actually making a chronic problem like an addiction worse.

The term *enabler* is also part of the larger definition of codependency.

Chapter 13

Watch Your wallet

If you have a crack head living with you, make sure you have a secure place to keep your valuables. I have a wall safe and a floor safe. I make sure when I don't have my valuables on my person they are in one of the safes. My wallet and credit cards, jewelry, watch, and cash are stored in the wall safe, and anything bigger is stored in the floor safe. Nothing is left out where it can be stolen. Before I got the safes, I used to keep my cash and wallet under the mattress on my side of the bed. I also make sure that when I take my pants off at night everything is removed and put in one of the safes. I have had too many things disappear while I have been sleeping. I have notified all of my creditors that nobody is to charge anything on my credit cards except me.

Here are a few ways Amy has taken me:

Gas Credit Card—She got my gas credit card. She notified her friends and crack head buddies she was going to have a gas sale. One by one, her friends and buddies showed up at the gas station. She allowed them to fill their gas tanks and charged them ten dollars each. She then charged the actual amount of the gas on my credit card. When I got the credit card bill, there was a balance of over $2,500 on it. I don't know how much money she put in her pocket. I didn't know this was happening until I was notified by the credit card company that the balance had increased drastically. By then it was too late to do anything about the additional charges.

CDs—I belong to a music service club where I can buy CDs at discount prices. I normally order six or eight CDs at the club price of $6.99 each. I like having a good music collection so I have something to play when I have friends over. Before I order CDs, I solicit the opinion of a few people around me, like my sons, Amy, and a few close friends. I have built up a pretty good collection. A little while ago, I decided to check my collection. I had many CDs with no cases. That's a good way to ruin a CD. I got everything together and started putting the correct CDs in the correct cases. I even checked to be sure the correct CDs were in the correct cases. When I was done, I had twenty-three CD cases with no CD. That's over $160 worth of CDs that were missing. I couldn't believe it. Where could they have gone? I asked Amy, and she told me she takes them to listen to them in her car, but before she can bring them back, someone steals them from her car. I didn't believe that, so I checked with one of her friends. Amy sells those CDs for three to five dollars each to get money for crack. If they are new, she will pawn them for two dollars each. What a deal—I buy the CD; Amy sells it and keeps the money. I have no CD and no money.

Checks—Amy found my checkbook in my desk; she wrote seven checks and forged my name to the signature line. She made the checks out to her family and friends and had them cash them. Then they split the money. The total of all the checks was $3,375. I turned the matter over to my bank, and I hope they will reimburse me for the checks. If they do, then they will go after Amy, and I will be out of it. If they do not reimburse me, I will have to sue Amy myself in civil court. It will be a hard case to win, because in Indiana a wife cannot steal from her husband. It is assumed that what is his is hers and vice versa. The bank will not have this problem, because they are not married to her. Amy is lucky—had this happened in most other states, she could have been charged criminally for forgery and check fraud.

Cash—Money is not safe in this house. If Amy finds it, it is gone, and so is Amy. I know Amy goes through my pants pockets when I go to sleep. I have to hide all my money and my wallet. She will take any money I have and a credit card or two from my wallet. She will spend the money on crack and buy things for her friends and sell it to them at a huge discount. That way she gets cash out of the credit cards. I am left to pay the bill. Again, I can't prosecute her because she is my wife.

Laptop Computer—I bought a new laptop computer along with a printer, carrying case, and scanner. The total of all the pieces was just under a thousand dollars. I had the bag and computer in the back of my van. Amy took my van without permission because her car was being worked on. She kept the van and was gone for the weekend. At some point, she found the computer. She sold it and all the extras for $150. Again, I couldn't do anything about it because she was my wife and the computer was marital property.

Food and Alcohol—Whenever Amy decides to disappear, she loads up all the food and alcohol she can carry out of this house. She is so slick, I never see it go. She goes so fast, I never know she is gone until after she has left. I never miss the items she took until I go to look for them. By then it is too late. I can remember one night when I was cooking dinner. I thought Amy was in the living room, and I was talking to her. When she didn't answer me, I went into the living room to see what the matter was. Amy was gone, and so was her car. I went back into the kitchen and found that all the booze and some of the food from the refrigerator was also gone. I had no idea why she left; she just did. She has done the same thing at night while we are sleeping. I roll over and see the lump under the blankets, but when I go to touch her, I find out that she is gone.

Cars—Amy has taken each of my two cars at least once. She will wait until I am not looking, then she will take off in the car. When she takes a car, she is normally gone for four days to a week. I have a BMW Z4 roadster with a high-power engine. When she takes that car, I worry. That is more power than she can handle. She will get into trouble or get hurt, not to mention what she can do to the car. Amy does not care what she does to the car; she thinks if she hurts the car, I will just fix it. She has been seen doing around 80 mph on neighborhood streets. Amy has no fear for what could happen; she knows they can't do much to her because she doesn't have anything. It will all come down on me.

I don't know why Amy does these things to me. I try to be nice to her. I try to give her whatever she needs. She has no reason to steal from me. Sometimes I wonder if Amy even knows why she does these things. I think she steals just to be stealing.

The need for crack is strong. It will cause the crack head to do things and take chances she normally wouldn't take. If she gets caught, she will try to lie her way out of it. The urge for crack is stronger than the fear of getting caught. She will do anything to get money for crack when she needs it.

Tonight, I was sitting in the recliner watching TV. I closed my eyes and was resting; I wasn't sleeping. Amy snuck up behind the recliner and tried to get my money from my pocket while I was sitting there. I was awake enough to feel it, and I caught her. Of course she tried to lie her way out of it. She said she was trying to wake me to be with her. She did this twice. She must really be in need of crack tonight. I made her leave the house. She will get the money somewhere; they always do.

One thing that helps me accept this is that I know I am not the only one Amy has done this to. She does the same thing to everyone whenever she spends time with them. She has stolen from her mother, her daughter, and her sister. Amy steals from everyone. She is an equal-opportunity thief. She has several charges of theft on her criminal record.

Chapter 14

Liar, Liar, Pants on Fire!

Amy is a perpetual liar. She lies about everything. She will even lie when telling the truth is better than the lie. She is so convincing with her lies that you cannot tell when she is telling the truth. I cannot tell when Amy is lying. And she will stick to her story to the death.

Amy will do what she wants then make up a story to cover her lie. When I call her in the car, she continually gives me a fabricated location. She never tells me the truth. If I ask her where she is, she will make up a place completely away from where she is. I wish I could put a GPS device on her car. She tells so many lies and fabricates so many stories that I am suspicious of what she is doing and with whom. Amy hasn't spent an entire week with me in months. She spends two or three days and nights away every week. That makes me wonder where she is and who she is with. Where is she spending her nights? I am tempted to put a private detective on her to see where she goes. Or I could get a rental car and do it myself. I am just tired of all the lies and fabrications. This is the nature of a crack head. She could be in a crack house for the night.

Here is a good example of how Amy can lie. I was home the other day. Amy asked me if I would use one of my credit cards and pay her cell phone bill for her. I said I would. I knew my wallet was on the dining room table, so I asked Amy to bring it to me so I could get the credit card and pay the bill. When she brought me the wallet, a credit card was missing. I asked her about the missing credit card, and she said it was on the table. I know it wasn't on the table when I put my wallet there. I didn't understand how my credit card got out of my wallet and onto the table. Credit cards do not have legs.

Here is one that happens all the time. I went to work this morning. Amy was still in bed when I left. She called me and left a message that she was going to spend the afternoon with her daughter and grandchildren. That would normally be okay. She should spend time with them. However, later that day, she was not answering her phone. I called her son-in-law and found out her daughter was working. I drove to her daughter's job to confirm that she was working. Amy was not with her daughter and never was. Why would she lie to me? Where is she, and who is she with? What is she doing? If she weren't a crack head, I would suspect another man, but with a crack head the crack means more than anything else. She was probably getting high somewhere.

Here is a favorite one Amy uses all the time. In fact she used it tonight while I was writing this chapter in this book.
I decided to take Amy out to listen to some music and have a few drinks tonight. I have to be careful when I do this, because Amy has a very low tolerance for alcohol. Normally, two or three drinks, and it is time to take Amy home. We were having a good time, and I wasn't paying attention to how strong the bartender was making her drinks. A strong drink is, sometimes, worse than a weak drink. A good bartender will make a drink according to the recipe and make it the same way each time.

Anyway, before I knew it, Amy was smashed. This is not a good thing for Amy, because the next step, for her, is crack cocaine. I finished my drink as fast as I could and took Amy home. Although she was drunk, we stopped for something to eat. When we got home Amy laid down on the couch and watched TV. I went into my office and was working on this book. I kept talking to her while I was going to the kitchen to get something to eat. I noticed the lump under the blankets on the couch. I went over to the lump and was going to give Amy a kiss good night. I pulled the blanket back and was shocked to see that Amy was not there. I immediately looked for her car. It was gone. Amy had left. I called her on the phone. She said she wanted some ice cream and was going to get some. That was a lie; she was going to get some crack. I told her to find someplace to stay because she couldn't come back here. I would deal with it in the morning.

Once Amy sets her story, she will go to the grave with that story. Her story cannot be shaken. I honestly believe she feels so strongly about the lies that she tells that she believes them herself. Once she has fabricated a lie in her mind, it becomes the truth.

This is how strongly she believes her lies. One afternoon she was sitting on the couch with her back to the hallway. As I came down the hallway, I saw her dial her phone and put it up to her ear. When the person she was calling answered she said, "Pedro? How are you?" At that point I was right behind her and asked, "Who are you talking to?" She hung up the phone and said, "My daughter. I was telling her about this guy named Pedro who was in the car when I blew out the tire." That's how easy crack heads can lie and expect the world to believe it. To them, it is protection, not a lie. Don't forget they are paranoid and believe everyone is out to get them.

Chapter 15

Always Has Crack!

No matter when or where, Amy seems to always have crack on her or knows where she can get it really quickly. Amy keeps track of where the drug is and how much it costs. She will take chances when others won't. Amy will do a hit of crack anytime and anywhere. The police can be all around her, but Amy will still get in and out with her crack. She can always get high when she wants to, and she keeps it a secret if she has any crack on her. The drug is precious to her, and she does not want to share.

That is a trait of a crack head. Everything crack heads do is secret. I would suppose that is mainly because everything they do is illegal. They have to keep everything closed up and behind locked doors.

Amy seems to be living two lives—one life with me and one life with the crack. The big problem comes when the two lives overlap and she can't do one of them. That is when I lose and the crack wins. Amy will always leave me sitting while she is off doing her crack. She seems to enjoy the excitement of skirting the law while she does her thing and gets high.

Chapter 16

Total Disregard for the Law

Amy has a total disregard for the law. She is not afraid of the police, jail, or prison. She feels she is smarter than the entire police department and they can't do anything to her. When she goes to jail or prison, that is like a badge of honor to her. The more times she is busted and goes away, the harder she gets and the more she is respected by her peers.

Yesterday I bailed Amy out of jail. I don't know why I did that; I shouldn't have. I should have let her sit in jail all weekend, but I felt sorry for her and bailed her out. She was okay last night because she didn't have a car; her car had been impounded. She stayed at her mom's house and didn't get into trouble. Today she got her car out of impound and rode around in it. Her driver's license was suspended by the court and the car is not safe to drive; yet, she is still riding around everywhere. She doesn't care if she gets pulled over. Tom will bail her out.

I can remember the night she got busted. Someone had turned Amy in because she had a warrant on her. Amy was in a crack house smoking crack, and the informant gave the police the exact address. I was in the crack house with her. When the police came, they knocked on the door and asked for her by name. Amy was sitting on a stool right behind the door, hitting on her crack pipe. When the police came, she kept hitting on that pipe like they weren't even there. Nobody would acknowledge knowing her or if she was there. Finally, the police came in to look for her. They didn't bother anybody else; they were just looking for Amy. When they started to leave, Amy figured they would find her behind the door, so she threw her pipe into the trash and stood up for them to take her. They took her outside and handcuffed her. It amazed me that Amy was so calm and acted like this was not a big deal. Of course this was not her first arrest or incarceration.

A Break in The Action
In-Law Joke

Q. Do you know the difference between in-laws and out-laws?
A. Outlaws are wanted.

Take that joke to your next family reunion.

Chapter 17

Living by the Wrong Clock

Amy is living by the wrong clock. She is awake when normal people are sleeping and sleeping when normal people are awake. That is the nature of her disease. Her day starts at around ten at night and ends around five in the morning. By 7:00 a.m. she is coming down off of her high and is getting ready to go to sleep. She will sleep until around four or five in the afternoon and then start all over again around ten. Illness is ever present in crack heads because of their lifestyle.

When I am looking for Amy, I don't even start until around eleven at night. Until then, she will be visiting some friends and setting up her buys for the night. She will not be out on the street. Around midnight she will start moving around and will be easier to find. She will be out looking around to see who has crack that she can get a hit of. At that point she will sell what she has to and do what she has to, to get the money for the crack that she needs. Nothing is sacred when she needs a fix.

In the beginning, I was worried and upset that she may be turning tricks and having sex with strange men to get the money for her crack. It really upset me. My wife may have been having sex with other men. Then I had a discussion with her probation officer. She told me, "Tom, don't be upset by what she may be doing. There is no emotion there. She has no feeling for the other person, nor he for her. She is strictly using one of the few assets she has in order to get the money she needs to support her habit." That didn't take away all of the worry and hurt, but it helped me a little bit.

Living life as a crack head isn't easy. Aside from being flip-flopped with the rest of the world on the time thing, crack heads have trouble functioning in the real world because they sleep when they should be awake. Important appointments are often missed, family functions are missed, and there is little or no interaction with loved ones.

It is also hard to be married to a crack head. Every night when I go to sleep, I wonder if she will still be there when I wake up. I wake up often through the night just to check and see if she is still there. Many nights she is not. And when she is gone, it is hard dealing with not knowing where she is or when she will be home. Sometimes she is gone for a day, and sometimes she is gone for a week. During the time she is gone, there are few phone calls or any other kind of interaction. The crack is the most important thing in her life, and I am second. Her lifestyle has put an extreme amount of stress on our marriage. I have filed for a divorce twice since we have been married. Twice I withdrew it. I made up my mind I cannot continue to be married to and involved with a crack head. The stress and turmoil is too much for me.

Chapter 18

My Ignorance

As I said in the introduction, I grew up in the sixties. I went to a large high school, with 610 students in my graduating class. Even in a school that size, drugs were almost completely unheard of. As I think back, I can only think of a few people who smoked marijuana. There certainly wasn't anybody within my immediate sphere of influence that used it. Cocaine was a drug that was used by the celebrity upper class. To my knowledge there was no crack cocaine at the time. I never knew drugs to be a major problem in my school.

Although this is a good thing, it also left me without a database to draw on regarding drugs, specifically crack cocaine. All I knew of that drug was that it was there. I never tried it, nor did I know anybody who had tried it. For that purpose, I am including a list of ways you can tell if someone is on crack cocaine.

How to Tell if Someone Is on Crack Cocaine

Unlike the cocaine it comes from, crack cocaine is solid rather than powdered. This is done so it can be smoked, which is the fastest way to get the drug into the bloodstream. Crack cocaine is a highly addictive drug that threatens the health of the individual user. Crack heads are known to have a greater incidence of health problems, including heart and lung damage. Individual crack cocaine users often exhibit certain behaviors that you can identify.

Symptoms of Crack Cocaine Use

1. Look at the eyes. Crack cocaine causes the pupils to dilate. Check the pupils; large pupils can be a sign of recent crack use.
2. Listen to the person's speech. If it is rapid and excitable or if their speech is inappropriate for the situation, that could be a sign of recent crack use.
3. Pay attention to the person's demeanor. Crack causes excitability and agitation in the user. If a person is normally relaxed but appears unable to sit still or concentrate, this may be a sign of recent crack usage. If the person appears agitated, it is possible the drug is wearing off.
4. Look for personality changes. A crack user will show marked changes in personality. They will become hostile and antagonistic to friends and family members. Their sleep patterns will change, and they may display signs of extreme paranoia. When under the influence of crack, they may act euphoric or manic, but as the drug wears off, they become sullen, withdrawn and depressed.
5. Examine the person's personal habits. A crack user will change their personal habits, including eating and grooming. They will often suffer rapid weight loss from lack of eating and care little about personal appearance and cleanliness.
6. Keep an eye on your valuables. The highly addictive nature of crack often influences users to acquire money at all costs. If you notice money or valuables missing from your home, it may indicate that a person in your home has started to use crack.
7. Keep your eyes open for drug paraphernalia. Since crack is most commonly smoked, be aware of the sudden appearance of glass pipes or an excessive number of lighters.

I submit education is the key. I can use my case as an example. I am a product of the sixties, when there was no crack cocaine. I could not be educated as to what crack cocaine was and what it could do to a person.

A lot of credit for my drug education must be given to my son and step-son. Both of my boys experimented with drugs. I think between alcohol and drugs, they tried everything known to man. At times, their mother and I were very worried, wondering if they were going to survive their drug use. Today, both of them have several years of a clean and sober lifestyle. We are thankful to God for watching over them and keeping them out of harm's way.

I remember Amy telling me she used crack cocaine. I thought, *Yeah, so she does some drugs.* I never put any emphasis on it because I didn't know what it was. To me a drug is a drug; they are all the same. Little did I know what I was getting myself into. I didn't know the toll it was going to take on my life and the life of Amy. Had I known, things might be different today. It's a shame there are no educational classes available for parents before their children go down the wrong path. In my house we had continual drug education and it still fell short of keeping my boys off of drugs. Peer pressure is much stronger than parental pressure. Unfortunately the "try me once and you will see" philosophy sometimes leads to a complete addiction.

Chapter 19

Crack Heads Are Irresponsible

It's time for me to vent. I have been polite and courteous through the whole first part of this book; now, it's time for me to tell you how I really feel.

I don't like crack heads. They are rude, uncaring, self-centered, and irresponsible. They don't care about anyone except themselves. They are so used to being loners that they forget all about other people. I have tried, on several occasions, to get close to a crack head and found it is not possible.

Tonight was a prime example of what I have to put up with from Amy. Amy had to clean out her storage locker or they would change the lock. She had known for two weeks that this had to be done. I told her I would help her if she needed me to, but she said she didn't need my help.

Around two this afternoon, her brother Timmy called. He is the worst crack head of all of them. He will tell you openly that he likes crack and has no intention of ever quitting it. He has been in and out of prison more than anyone in the family. Timmy likes to take Amy with him when he does crack because her looks and personality can get the drug when he can't. I asked Amy not to hang around with him because he is trouble. She won't listen to me and continues to be with him. Amy went to get Timmy this afternoon and never came back. Timmy has an influence over Amy because he is her big brother. He uses her, but she doesn't see it.

Amy continually steals things from me to give to Timmy. I know he has at least two of my knives, or at least he had them at one time. Timmy comes in here but doesn't have the nerve to steal anything, so he has his sister do it for him.

So never depend on a crack head to do anything for you. They are irresponsible and undependable.

It wasn't too long ago that I had a small stroke while sitting at home. I was on the floor and couldn't get up. I needed help, and I needed it immediately. Amy had left earlier in the day, and I had no idea where she was. Fortunately, she had her cell phone with her. If she just had it turned on, I would be able to reach her and get help. I tried her number, and she answered the phone. I told her what had happened and that I needed help. I could tell she was high. She told me she would be home in a little over an hour and to hang in there until she got there. I couldn't believe she was putting me off for crack cocaine. I was in a serious, life-threatening position, and she couldn't take the time away from the crack to come and help me.

I called my son, and he was there within ten minutes. We called 911, and I went to the hospital. They diagnosed me as having a small stroke, stabilized me, and sent me home. Amy never did show up. She didn't come home for three days.

Amy turns her phone off when she goes to bed. She normally doesn't go to bed until around four or five in the morning, and she doesn't wake up until around two in the afternoon. That means she is not reachable most of the day.

I spoke to Amy around two today. I asked her if she would like to come over to the house and hang out. She said yes, and she would be here around two thirty. Amy called me at three thirty and told me she was running late but would be here for sure. At six, she still hadn't showed up. She had her phone turned off, so I couldn't reach her. Crack heads are irresponsible!

Always have a contingency plan in effect if you have a crack head in the house. In case of emergency, you cannot depend upon a crack head.

For all of her bad features, Amy has twice that amount in good features. She is obviously a very attractive young lady. She has a good job and a good car. She is professional in her dealings with the public, and many more good things.

Chapter 20

Always Second, Never First

To a crack head, the most important thing in the world is crack cocaine. Nothing—I repeat, *nothing*—comes before crack. That includes family, friends, food, work, and scheduled activities such as sporting events or shows. Crack will always come before any other activity.

As I mentioned, Amy does not have custody of any of her children. Since she does not have custody, she has visitation rights (also known as Parenting Time). Provided she is current with her other obligations to her children, she can have visitation with her children every Wednesday evening and every other weekend from Friday night to Sunday night. Amy normally calls and sets up visitation on the weekends. She starts out wanting to pick up the children as soon as they are ready to go, but then the problems start.

Friday night is a prime night for crack users and abusers everywhere. There are new batches of crack available for good prices. If Amy has her children at the house, how can she be out with her crack head friends? Easy—she will leave her children with me or some other relative and go on her way. Remember, crack comes first.

Another problem comes into play after she gets high. When Amy is high, she does not want to come down. She normally stays high until her money, and possibly other assets, run out. At times like that, depending on how much money she has, she doesn't come home until sometime after noon on Saturday. She can't do that when she has her children at home. But when she is high none of that matters. Don't forget—crack comes first. Amy will continue to do her thing without regard for her visitation with her children. She will just not show up.

I have seen weekends when Amy would be there to see her children arrive for visitation. She would spend around an hour with them, then she would make up an excuse and leave. That would be the last they would see of her for the weekend. She would be off doing her thing without regard for who was waiting at home for her. Don't forget—crack comes first. She forgets all about her children when she is high on crack cocaine. All she is thinking about is how is she going to get her next hit or piece of a rock.

These last couples of days have been typical for Amy and her crack. Today is Wednesday morning. On Monday afternoon, I took a nap. When I awoke, Amy was gone. She left no note or message of any kind say where she went or when she would return. This is typical for Amy; when she leaves, she just leaves. I called her, and she said she was going to clean out her storage locker, and that she was going to get her brother Timmy so he could help her. This was trouble; there is always trouble when Timmy is around. I told her I was making baked chicken for dinner and it would be ready around six thirty, and I asked her to please be on time. Amy said she was hungry, and she would be here on time. Well, six thirty came and went, and Amy never showed up. Dinner was ruined, and I had to throw it out.

Amy did not come home at all on Monday night. I called her Tuesday morning, and she said she had spent the night in her car. I don't know where she was, but I don't believe she slept in her car. I asked her if she was coming home on Tuesday, and she said yes. I started to make breakfast, but I stopped because I didn't want to waste more food if she didn't show up.

Just as I thought, Amy never showed up on Tuesday. I'm glad I didn't cook breakfast. If you haven't figured it out, I do all of the cooking in our household. Amy cannot cook very well, or at least I won't eat what she cooks.

While Amy wasn't here, she was drunk and high most of the time. There was a price for that. She hit the curb with her right front tire and blew it out. She managed to get someone to help her put the donut on so she could drive the car, but she needed another tire to put on. I told her to get a price on a tire and let me know. She didn't do it; instead, she drove around with the donut. Then, on Tuesday afternoon, she got drunk and hit the curb again—this time with the donut. Now she needs a real tire and rim and a donut and rim. I am running out of money helping her. I should just make her handle it herself. I can't keep paying for everything for her.

I am waiting on a price for a tire and rim.

Crack heads want, or need, the high that goes along with alcohol or drugs. They are so used to having that feeling that they miss it when it is not there. This is what they call withdrawal, which we will get into in a later chapter. Getting that tire and rim was not a priority item for Amy. She would only get into that if she could get the buzz back. Now she was off looking for some way to get drunk or high. I wouldn't hear from her until she had what she wanted.

I finally heard from Amy. She was high. Funny how she didn't have money to fix her car, but she could always find a way to get high when she wanted to. Just like I said, "Everything else is second; crack is first."

I'm not always second. Recently, Amy and I spent the day together. She slept most of the day, and I wrote more of the book. That was okay; I got lots done on the book. When she woke up, we went to get her car at the motel. Remember, her brother took a knife to her tire. I was uncomfortable going to that motel, but I went anyway. I told her how I felt about picking her up at a motel. I thought she understood, but as I write this, I'm thinking maybe she didn't understand. I tried to tell her how I felt about the way she was treating me and that, if she wanted me, she would have to change. She said she would try. I was happy with the conversation we had.

During our conversation, Amy told me she would like to have filet mignon on the grill for dinner. I knew it was expensive, about twenty-five dollars a pound, but I got it for her anyway. I was going to make a nice dinner for her. I set the table outside, including flowers, and waited for her to come home. Amy called me and told me where she was and that she was on her way home. I got everything ready to go except for putting the meat on the grill. I waited. Amy never showed up. She obviously had something she wanted to do more, so she put me second and just didn't show up.

I was really upset by the way Amy was treating me. All of her friends are more important than I am. She will let me down continually, but she will always be there for her crack head friends.

For some stupid reason, I decided to give Amy a second chance. I bought another filet mignon the next night and set everything up like I had the night before. I was going to be nice one more time. Guess what? She stood me up again. I must be the dumbest person on the planet. When I called her to ask why she didn't show up, she said because she was with Suzie and they were talking. I sat at home waiting on her, and she was talking with Suzie. That's why I say I am always second and never first.

The definition of insanity is often said to be doing the same thing the same way over and over and expecting different results. I must be insane!

What goes around comes around, like karma. Before me Amy had a long-term relationship with a nice guy named Kent. Amy loved Kent, and he loved her. They were together for over four years and had two children, both girls. For the most part, they had a very happy relationship. They never got married. The main problem they had was Amy's continual use of crack cocaine. She was a heavy user and would not get off of it. Just like with me, she would neglect Kent. He always came second to the crack. Her use of crack cocaine took its toll on their relationship.

Kent worked the midnight shift in a jewelry factory. When he left for work, Amy would have a babysitter lined up. She would follow him out the driveway shortly thereafter. She would return home before he got home from work. I am told there were nights when Amy couldn't find a babysitter, so she would leave the children alone and go and pick up a piece of a rock and smoke it at home. It got so bad that Kent used to put soft drink cans behind her tires so she would crush them when she moved the car while he was at work. That way he knew if she had left or not. Kent tried to do everything he could to keep his relationship with Amy going and provide a home for his family. Amy was not helping him.

Finally, out of complete frustration, Kent turned to Amy's family for help. He felt that maybe one of her siblings might be able to talk some sense to her. He found one of her sisters, Loretta, who wanted to help. Now here is the karma part: He took Loretta to a motel so they could talk in private and nobody would know. Well, Amy caught them and dumped him. He still swears that nothing happened; they were just talking. Now Amy gets caught in a motel, and she swears nothing happened. If that's not karma, I don't know what is. Amy lost a long-term relationship because of a motel room, and now she is about to lose me for the same reason. If she would have just believed and trusted in Kent, they would still be together, and I wouldn't have ever met Amy.

Here's the icing on the cake. When we left the room I was the last one to leave. I looked around before I left. There was a condom wrapper on the floor and a wet spot on the bed. How was Amy going to explain those things? This would be interesting. Amy knows every answer in the book, and she is a good liar. Let's see how she got out of this one. I knew what I saw, and I knew what that meant.

I asked Amy about the condom wrapper and the wet spot in the bed. The only answer she would give me was that she didn't know anything about them because she didn't do anything. She just kept sticking to that story. Remember, one of the traits of crack heads is that they are good liars.

I hope you can see that life with a crack head is not easy. I am not sure I can blame the drug for all of this. It seems like a great deal of our problems stem directly from personality traits. Which brings up another question: is personality learned or inherited? The answer may have to wait for another book. However, I will leave it open with these possibilities:

1. There are two people who are directly involved in both inherited personality traits and learned, or taught, personality traits. Father and mother.
2. Should one or both of these people be responsible, in whole or in part, for the outcome of their children? Absolutely!
3. Should parenting classes be required for all expecting parents? How about continuing education during the early personality-forming, years? Yes!

I have heard it said, and I believe it to be true, "What an awesome responsibility we have, as a parent, to be the role model for the person we most want our children to become." If I had my way, I would make every prospective parent sign that statement and agree to be responsible for their children for life. Too many people think parenting stops when the child reaches eighteen years of age. That's not true. That's when it becomes the hardest. That's when they need a parent the most.

Should a parent be able to divorce and walk away from their children? Absolutely not. Both parents should be required to stay in the home until all of the children are raised and have demonstrated their ability to live on their own without any law enforcement intervention for a period of five years.

PARENTING IS A LIFELONG PROPOSITION!

Chapter 21

The Liability Is Yours

Let's get down to a very serious part of being married to a crack head: the liability you have for your crack head wife's actions. I am not an attorney or an insurance agent, and I am not giving advice in either area. I am merely trying to point out some of the pitfalls you may not be aware of when you marry a crack head. I highly suggest you consult your attorney and insurance agent to see if the same applies to you as it does to me.

I am ashamed to say Amy does not have any automobile insurance. I have argued that she must have it by law in our state, but she does not want to pay for it. She feels it is a waste of money because it probably wouldn't cover an accident if she was under the influence of alcohol or drugs. Her car is in her name alone, and I do not drive it. I have done everything I can to disassociate myself from that car.

There is one final drastic thing you can do. You can get a divorce. I have a home, some cars, and other assets that I must protect. I have children from previous marriages whom I must also protect. I cannot allow Amy to jeopardize what I have worked my whole life to obtain. I love Amy very much and, although she has some serious faults, I still want her at my side. I hope someday she will be able to put this all behind us and live a normal life. We plan on staying together and living together after the divorce is final.

Again, I am not giving legal or insurance advice, but please check with the professionals you deal with and protect yourself if you are married to a crack head.

There is one other thing to consider. If Amy gets arrested or hurt and is taken to the hospital, the expenses are yours. They will bill her first; but when she can't pay for it, they will come directly to you for payment. This is only true if you are married. If you are not married they will stop with her.

Chapter 22

Seek Professional Help!

I cannot say this enough—if you are married to or have control over a person who is addicted to crack cocaine, *seek professional help!* This is not something to put off; do it today! And when you get help, don't only get it for the crack head; get help for yourself also. Dealing with a crack head on a daily basis is not an easy thing to do, and it takes its toll on your health. See your doctor and let him know what you are doing.

Drug addiction is a serious disease, and addition to crack cocaine is the top of the ladder. Crack cocaine can, and often times does, kill the user. I have been with Amy when she did a hit of crack. I monitored her heart rate before, during, and after her use. Her heart rate went up three times its normal rate while she was on it. That's a substantial increase. When she uses, it goes up fast, levels off at the increased rate, then comes down slowly. The heart rate does not come down as quickly as it went up. This all contributes to damage and increased wear on the heart.

There are some really good rehab centers that can, and will be more than happy to, help the crack head. But the user has to want to do it. It's not enough that we want them to quit; they have to want to do it themselves. They have to be committed to the rehab program.

This is what happens if they are not committed to the rehab program. My stepson Jerry was the worst drug user in our family. He used or experimented with any drug he could find. He was always high. His mother and I were very worried about him. His mother kept harping about rehab, but Jerry was too busy drinking and drugging to worry about it. For a young, single male, he had it made. He was the leader of his pack. The only real problem he had was that his lifestyle was killing him

Finally, the day came when Jerry was having a bad day and his mother was harping on rehab and he agreed to go. Not because he wanted to, but because he thought he should to make his mother feel better. And especially not because he thought it would help him. He was going for the wrong reason. He was going because his mother wanted him to go.

I went to visit Jerry while he was in rehab. It was a joke. He took me on a tour of the facility. He had everything a young man could want. He had a pool table, game room, exercise room, and a refrigerator stocked with snacks all he could ever want. And it was an open-door facility. If he ever decided he didn't like it, he could leave. He told me, "This isn't a bad place to hang out for the next six weeks." He was not taking this rehab seriously.

Jerry went through the program, didn't cause any trouble, and made his mother happy. He should have been able to get off of drugs and stay clean. There was only one reason he didn't: Jerry didn't want to quit doing drugs. Jerry liked his lifestyle. So, Jerry left the rehab facility around four one afternoon and was back using crystal meth by ten that night. The program was a total failure for Jerry.

I don't want to leave this on a sour note. For the next few years, Jerry continued on with his alcohol and drug career. He had graduated to daily use of crystal meth. Jerry was a free spirit. He didn't work or sleep. He was losing weight fast. Personal hygiene became a thing of the past. The only things you could say about Jerry would have to be bad. He was dying a slow death due to the drugs. If there were a professional drug tour, like the golf tour, Jerry would qualify to be on it every week.

As Jerry was getting worse and worse, his mother and I were scouring the Midwest trying to find a place that would help him. Jerry was almost ready to give in and try rehab again. This time it would be because he wanted it.

Then it happened. One day Jerry called his mother and told her he was done with drugs and needed help. His mother and her husband sprang into action. They had found a place out of state that would take Jerry and help him to recover from his addiction. Jerry spent a year and a half in rehab in order to recover from his years of drug activity.

Happy Ending

Today Jerry has almost nine years of drug-free sobriety. He is married and has three wonderful children. He has a good job and just bought a new home to raise his children in. Jerry is an example of what can be done when you let go and accept help. We are all very proud of Jerry!

Chapter 23

Codependency

Codependency is a learned behavior that can be passed down from one generation to another. It is an emotional and behavioral condition that affects an individual's ability to have a healthy, mutually satisfying relationship. It is also known as "relationship addiction" because people with codependency often form or maintain relationships that are one-sided, emotionally destructive, and/or abusive. The disorder was first identified about ten years ago as the result of years of studying interpersonal relationships in families of alcoholics. Codependent behavior is learned by watching and imitating other family members who display this type of behavior.

Who Does Codependency Affect?

Codependency often affects a spouse, a parent, sibling, friend, or coworker of a person afflicted with alcohol or drug dependence. Originally, codependent was a term used to describe partners in chemical dependency, persons living with or in a relationship with an addicted person. Similar patterns have been seen in people in relationships with chronically or mentally ill individuals. Today, however, the term has broadened to describe any codependent person from any dysfunctional family.

What Is a Dysfunctional Family and How Does it Lead to Codependency?

A dysfunctional family is one in which members suffer from fear, anger, pain, or shame that is ignored or denied. Underlying problems may include any of the following:

- An addiction by a family member to drugs, alcohol, relationships, work, food, sex, or gambling.
- The existence of physical, emotional, or sexual abuse.
- The presence of a family member suffering from a chronic mental or physical illness.

Dysfunctional families do not acknowledge that problems exist. They don't talk about them or confront them. As a result, family members learn to repress emotions and disregard their own needs. They become "survivors." They develop behaviors that help them deny, ignore, or avoid difficult emotions. They detach themselves. They don't talk. They don't touch. They don't confront. They don't feel. They don't trust. The identity and emotional development of the members of a dysfunctional family are often inhibited.

Attention and energy focus on the family member who is ill or addicted. The codependent person typically sacrifices his or her needs to take care of a person who is sick. When codependents place other people's health, welfare, and safety before their own, they can lose contact with their own needs, desires, and sense of self.

How Do Codependent People Behave?

Codependents have low self-esteem and look for anything outside of themselves to make them feel better. They find it hard to "be themselves." Some try to feel better through alcohol, drugs, or nicotine and become addicted. Others may develop compulsive behaviors like workaholism, gambling, or indiscriminate sexual activity.

They have good intentions. They try to take care of a person who is experiencing difficulty, but the caretaking becomes compulsive and defeating. Codependents often take on a martyr's role and become "benefactors" to an individual in need. A wife may cover for her alcoholic husband; a mother may make excuses for a truant child; or a father may "pull some strings" to keep his child from suffering the consequences of delinquent behavior.

The problem is that these repeated rescue attempts allow the needy individual to continue on a destructive course and to become even more dependent on the unhealthy caretaking of the "benefactor." As this reliance increases, the codependent develops a sense of reward and satisfaction from "being needed." When the caretaking becomes compulsive, the codependent feels choiceless and helpless in the relationship, but is unable to break away from the cycle of behavior that causes it. Codependents view themselves as victims and are attracted to that same weakness in the love and friendship relationships.

Characteristics of Co-dependent People Are:

- An exaggerated sense of responsibility for the actions of others
- A tendency to confuse love and pity, with the tendency to "love" people they can pity and rescue
- A tendency to do more than their share, all of the time
- A tendency to become hurt when people don't recognize their efforts
- An unhealthy dependence on relationships. The codependent will do anything to hold on to a relationship to avoid the feeling of abandonment
- An extreme need for approval and recognition
- A sense of guilt when asserting themselves
- A compelling need to control others
- Lack of trust in self and/or others
- Fear of being abandoned or alone
- Difficulty identifying feelings
- Rigidity/difficulty adjusting to change
- Problems with intimacy/boundaries
- Chronic anger
- Lying/dishonesty
- Poor communications
- Difficulty making decisions

Questionnaire to Identify Signs Of Codependency

This condition appears to run in different degrees, whereby the intensity of symptoms are on a spectrum of severity, as opposed to an all-or-nothing scale. Please note that only a qualified professional can make a diagnosis of codependency; not everyone experiencing these symptoms suffers from codependency.

1. Do you keep quiet to avoid arguments?
2. Are you always worried about others' opinions of you?
3. Have you ever lived with someone with an alcohol or drug problem?
4. Have you ever lived with someone who hits or belittles you?
5. Are the opinions of others more important than your own?
6. Do you have difficulty adjusting to changes at work or home?
7. Do you feel rejected when significant others spend time with friends?
8. Do you doubt your ability to be who you want to be?
9. Are you uncomfortable expressing your true feelings to others?
10. Have you ever felt inadequate?
11. Do you feel like a "bad person" when you make a mistake?
12. Do you have difficulty taking compliments or gifts?
13. Do you feel humiliation when your child or spouse makes a mistake?
14. Do you think people in your life would go downhill without your constant efforts?
15. Do you frequently wish someone could help you get things done?
16. Do you have difficulty talking to people in authority, such as the police or your boss?
17. Are you confused about who you are or where you are going with your life?
18. Do you have trouble saying "no" when asked for help?
19. Do you have trouble asking for help?
20. Do you have so many things going at once that you can't do justice to any of them?

If you identify with several of these symptoms and are dissatisfied with yourself or your relationships, you should consider seeking professional help. Arrange for a diagnostic evaluation with a licensed physician or psychologist experienced in treating codependency.

How Is Codependency Treated?

Because codependency is usually rooted in a person's childhood, treatment often involves exploration into early childhood issues and their relationship to current destructive behavior patterns. Treatment includes education, experiential groups, and individual and group therapy through which codependents rediscover themselves and identify self-defeating behavior patterns. Treatment also focuses on helping patients getting in touch with feelings that have been buried during childhood and on reconstructing family dynamics. The goal is to allow them to experience their full range of feelings again.

When Codependency Hits Home

The first step in changing unhealthy behavior is to understand it. It is important for codependents and their family members to educate themselves about the course and cycle of addiction and how it extends into their relationships. Libraries, drug and alcohol abuse treatment centers, and mental health centers often offer educational materials and programs to the public.

A lot of change and growth is necessary for the codependent and his or her family. Any caretaking behavior that allows or enables abuse to continue in the family needs to be recognized and stopped. The codependent must identify and embrace his or her feelings and needs. This may include learning to say no, to be loving yet tough, and learning to be self-reliant. People find freedom, love, and serenity in their recovery.

Hope lies in learning more. The more you understand codependency, the better you can cope with its effects. Reaching out for information and assistance can help someone live a healthier, more fulfilling life.

Chapter 24

She Wants to Get Off of Crack!

I don't want to lead anyone into thinking Amy is a hopeless crack head. She is far from that. Amy would like to quit using crack really badly, but she doesn't know how. She is not the kind of person who takes help from anyone. Amy has been on her own and doing for herself since she was sixteen years old. She is a very independent person. It is hard for her to accept the fact that she may need help getting off of the crack.

Amy has been trying to get off of crack for nearly two years. It is hard for her because she has been doing it for so many years. Everyone she knows, except me, does crack. Her brother and her sisters do crack. Her cousins do crack. Her friends do crack. She is caught up in a crack universe. That makes it hard for her to quit. No matter how hard she tries, someone is always there offering her a hit or a rock. I do not see how she is going to quit while she is around her friends and family.

Amy may have to be like Jerry and move out of the area in order to get clean. If she does decide to move, it will take a tremendous amount of determination to stay clean. It will do no good to move and continue with the same behavior at the new place. If she continues to hit the bars and get drunk, she will eventually find the crack. She has to stay away from people, places, and things that make crack look attractive and available, and that includes alcohol. I'm afraid I may be more of a hindrance than a help. I drink, and I will have to stop that if I expect her to be successful. I love her so much I will do it for her, if I can.

She has to realize that, at least for the first year, she cannot come back to see her friends or family or contact them in any way. That would also mean telephone contact. Her old friends and family will be poison to her until she can turn down crack on her own. She will have to find a job and activities to occupy her time. She has to stay busy. It would be good for her to join a group like Alcoholics Anonymous or Narcotics Anonymous and become active. She will also need support from people other than me. She cannot do this on her own.

Interruption

Amy just came home. She was high and brought a piece of a rock with her. She went into the bathroom and smoked what she had left. I feel really let down. I wish she would go someplace for the rest of the night. I am tired, and I don't want to deal with her tonight.

After Amy took the wheel back to the person who lent it to her, she went to a bar in her old neighborhood. While she was there, one of her cousins came in. Her name is Carise, and she is a bad one. They sat at the bar and had a few beers, but the beer wasn't enough, so they got some crack and smoked it. That was only the start for Amy. She got some more crack and made an evening out of it.

So you see, when she left me earlier tonight, Amy was talking about trying to quit using crack. That all changed in an instant when she ran into her cousin. She has to get away from all of those people if she is ever going to have a chance at quitting the crack.

Amy is a good person at heart; she just got addicted to one of the worst drugs known to man. Someday she will figure out how to stop using it and this will all stop. I wish I could help her more, but I'm afraid I have done as much as I can for her. As much as I love her, I would be willing to give her up if that meant she could get off of the crack. I don't want to see her die from the crack. Amy has to hit rock bottom before she will be able to get off of crack cocaine. She has to know the feeling of having nothing because of the drug. She has to get sicker than she ever has before. This will never happen so long as Amy is with me because I will not allow it to happen. Amy must go for her own good. I must divorce Amy in order for her to get clean. It will be a hard thing for both of us to do, but it may be the only way she can get completely off of crack cocaine.

We all know she only has three ways to go if she stays on the crack: incarcerated, institutionalized, or dead. Harsh as they are, these are her only choices. God, please help her!

Chapter 25

Disappearing Act

Nobody agrees on everything all the time. Amy and I have our share of disagreements. Perhaps we argue more than normal. That may be because of the age and cultural differences we have. It is hard for us because we are so diverse. The good part is when we agree, we agree wholly.

I have found over the years, three marriages, and several serious relationships, it is always best to sit down and try to work out your differences. You cannot hide from them. You cannot run away from them—you have to work them out. If you don't at least try to work them out, they will still be there tomorrow and tomorrow and tomorrow, until you do at least discuss the problem.

Amy chooses to deal with our problems in a different way. She just flat refuses to deal with them. Instead she disappears. I don't mean she goes in the other room and closes the door; I mean "now you see her now you don't" disappearing. She is almost as good as Houdini.

This one always gets me. We will be in the living room discussing something important. We will not be arguing, but it will be a discussion that is not very comfortable for Amy. I will be sitting in the recliner, and Amy will be laying down on the couch with a blanket pulled over her. We will be talking normally. If I get up and leave the room, everything changes. When I come back, Amy will no longer talk to me. No matter what I say, she will not answer me. Finally out of frustration, I will go to the couch and pull the blanket off of her head so she has to look at me. When I do that, I find out she is not there. It is pillows under that blanket. I look at the front door and find it is unlocked. I go outside and look in the driveway; her car is gone. Amy has successfully disappeared. This is almost as good as David Copperfield making the Statue of Liberty disappear. She is good. She should be on the stage; it leaves on the corner in fifteen minutes, yuk, yuk!

(My brother used to live in Palisades Park, New Jersey. He lived in a high-rise condo on one of the upper floors. From his balcony, he could see the Statue of Liberty. One evening David Copperfield was on TV, and he was going to make the Statue of Liberty disappear. I called my brother and had him sit on his balcony and watch the statue. Guess what? The statue did not disappear. It sure did on TV, but from my brother's vantage point, it never went anywhere. Amazing what technology can do today. Just thought you might like to know that. Sorry David, I didn't mean to blow your secret.)

Here is one of her favorite ones and, damn it, it gets me almost every time. When we are home, Amy spends an inordinate amount of time in the hallway bathroom. She considers that her bathroom. Right across the hall from this bathroom door is the door to the laundry room and the garage and outside. Amy uses this bathroom to smoke her crack when she is in the house. When Amy is ready to sneak out of the house, she goes into this bathroom and turns on the light and fan. Although my back is to it, I can turn and see the bathroom door from my recliner if I turn around. I can see the light under the door, which is how I know if someone is in the bathroom. Amy will sit inside the bathroom and wait. When she thinks I am interested in the TV, she opens the bathroom door and slips across the hallway to the laundry room and eventually outside. She makes sure to leave the light and fan on and lock the door. In time I get tired of waiting for her, so I get up and start banging on the door. Of course nobody answers, because nobody is in there. Now I am suspicious. I run to get the little screwdriver that opens the door. I open the door and discover nobody is in there. Then it hits me. I turn around and notice the door from the laundry room to the garage is ajar. I go to the door and open the big garage door. There it is—an empty driveway. She successfully made it; she has disappeared.

When am I going to learn? Amy came over to the house, and I cooked a couple of steaks on the grill. Actually, Amy wanted filet mignon, at $24.99 a pound. I have been cooking fairly regularly on the grill, and I was afraid I was going to run out of gas. So I asked Amy to drive to the gas station and get a refill. I also gave her $20 for gas for her car and asked her to bring me a receipt. I went into the office and was working on this book. I fell asleep while I was on the computer. I woke up about twenty minutes later. I could tell Amy had been here, but she was gone now. She left the tank for the grill on the front porch and took off. She was in a hurry to get somewhere; I wonder where it was? This is the kind of treatment you get from a crack head.

In order of importance, here is the short list for a crack head:

1. Crack
2. Themselves
3. You

Chapter 26

Continually Left Alone

There is nothing worse than being married and being lonely. The hours seem like days, the days seem like weeks, and there is nothing you can do about it. Spousal neglect is the worst form of abuse there is. Sixty-five percent of all divorces are caused by some form of spousal neglect. A close second behind that is lack of communication. If you are not at home, it is hard to communicate with your spouse.

Solitary confinement was used as a form of punishment against POWs during World War II. Today solitary confinement is used in many prisons across the country. Make no mistake; when you take away a person's ability to interact with other people, you take away a part of what makes them a person.

Amy continually finds things to do with her friends and leaves me sitting at home alone, wondering where she is. When I try to call her, she will not answer her phone. She cares for no one but herself and her crack use comes before anything else. She refuses treatment. She refuses crack addiction help. Most everything she mutters is profane. Every second word out of her mouth starts with an "f".

Like the title says, I married to a crack head. Well, by legal definition I am married. I have a marriage license and a marriage certificate. But am I morally married? I am not sure.

It has been almost two years since the justice of the peace said we were married. Amy has not yet moved all of her things into our home. She keeps most of her things in the trunk of her car and lives out of her trunk. Most of her clothes and all of her important things are in that trunk. Her reasoning for not moving into my home is that I ask her to move out after she is there. That only happens when she crosses the line and does something wrong, like staying away for days without calling. Or bringing crack into my home.

Amy has never spent a full week in this house with me. The longest has been three days; then she is gone for a day or two. When she is gone, she never tells me where she is going. She just leaves without a good-bye or anything. Most times I will be talking to her, and she will stop talking. When I go to find out why she stopped talking, I usually find that she is gone. She usually won't answer her phone, or she will turn it off completely. This tells me she doesn't want to talk to me. Amy never calls me after she has gone; I have to call her if I want to talk to her. Once Amy leaves, she will never tell me where she is or if or when she will be back. She is afraid I will go after her and cause trouble.

I used to think she had another man she was seeing; now, I'm not sure. I am starting to think the other man is crack. I know from experience Amy is not amorous when she smokes crack. She normally has a "don't touch me" attitude after smoking crack.

Amy takes off for two to five days at a time and expects me to accept that. She continually leaves me alone while she is off doing her thing. This is not normal behavior for a married couple. However, this is normal behavior for a crack head. While on a binge, a crack head may stay away up for days at a time.

I am having a hard time getting her to understand what goes through my mind when she is gone like this. This morning Amy called me and had me pick her up at a motel room. When I asked who rented the room, she said a girlfriend did. How do I know that? All I know is I picked my wife up at a motel room. She had no money when she left yesterday, so who paid for the room? The motel said Amy paid for the room in cash. Who was in the room with her? It's hard to trust crack heads because of some of the things they do; it's even harder when they do things like this. A little bit of caring would go a long way in this situation. Crack heads will use whatever asset they have to get money when they don't have any. That is why I am concerned when she calls me from a motel room.

All people, not just crack heads, may be better off if they think of the effects of their behavior on other people. A good book to read is Dale Carnegie's book *How to Win Friends, and Influence People.*

Chapter 27

Crack Addiction Help

The hardest part about help is getting it, even though there is a lot of help available. It's hard because the crack addict does not *want* help. They want to be *left alone*. They know they don't have a problem, and they want everyone to *mind their own business!*

Their families see it, but it doesn't matter.
Their friends see it.
Their coworkers see it.
They don't see it. Everybody else is wrong!

Actually, it is important that the addict see the problem. Without the buy-in of the addict, without him or her realizing they have a serious problem, no treatment is going to take place. They will refuse to get help to matter what!

There is a television reality show called *Intervention* that documents the denial of addicts as they are approached by family and friends to seek help. In one episode, the crack addict who is destroying her health, her family's property, and all of her relationships is steadfastly in denial that there is any problem of any kind and refuses crack addiction help.

She curses her family for bringing it up. She cares for no one but herself, and her crack use comes before anything else. She refuses treatment. She refuses crack addiction help. Most everything she mutters is profane. She is completely lost.

The wake left behind a crack addict is the crushed hearts of those who see the problem and want to help, but for the best of reasons, they likely contribute to the problem rather than solve it. In these shows, an interventionist is called in by the family, not just to confront the addict and coax them into rehabilitation, but to coach the family and teach them communication skills.

Crack addiction help is not based on enabling the addict; once rules are established, they *must* be adhered to. If the rules are broken, the addict *must* feel the consequences; otherwise, the family is going to *enable* the addict to continue using. No crack addiction help is possible!

Crack addiction is not just a family problem; it's a community problem. Help from the community is a necessary ingredient for any addict achieving recovery. Families are too close to the addict. They love that person, they care, they cry for them. Their loving regard for the addict blocks their objective thinking and prevents them from being the answers to the problem. They become enablers and feed the problem. Crack addiction help from a professional is needed to treat all parties involved in the addiction.

Once the family and friends are onboard with the need for professional help and new communication patterns and boundaries are established by the professional, "their" problem will become the addict's problem. Once the addict realizes that they have the problem, the first step towards recovery is taken.

Chapter 28

A Leopard Doesn't Change It's Spots!

It's 2:00 a.m. on Friday night/Saturday morning. Amy just called me from the jail. They just released her. She needs a ride home or wherever she wants to go. My first thought was to tell her no and to find someone else. Then I remembered all the nice letters she sent me saying how she was going to stop drinking and stop doing drugs. I couldn't just give up on her if she was going to get clean and sober and stay that way. But, is she clean and will she stay that way?

In the last week Amy has done nothing to improve herself or prepare for life without crack cocaine. She has made no effort to find a job or a place to live. Even if we stay together, she is not prepared to uphold her end of the relationship. Amy will be lost without me.

The night before Amy was due to be released from jail she called me and asked me to be sure I had a bottle of her favorite wine chilled when she got there. Remember, she promised me she wasn't going to drink when she got out of jail. I did as she asked and she drank the whole bottle in one sitting.

On Sunday night we went out to dinner. Amy had three Martinis after dinner. She wanted a fourth but I reminded her that she was trying to quit drinking.

On Monday night Amy was not home when I got home. There was no note saying where she was and I did not receive a phone call. Obviously Amy called someone and had them pick her up. She did not take her phone so I could not track her. Finally, Amy came home at 11:30 p.m. She did not see anything wrong with what she did. All she did was visit a girlfriend and nothing else. She neglected to remember to let me know where she was going and approximately when she would be back. She never had the time to call me and let me know where she was. When I asked if I could talk to this friend I was told no. When I asked where she lived, Amy did not know the address. Or, Amy said that the friend lived with her mom and her mom didn't want her to give the address out.

Last night was a really unique night. Amy took off while I was working on this chapter of the book. Only this time she left a note. The note said, "Gone to get Benadryl, be back soon." Now that little note set me laughing for ten minutes. The last time Amy went to get Benadryl she got a ticket for her second OWI in a one-week period and did not come home for over 120 days. And, that time, she was not going for Benadryl; she was going to meet someone to buy crack. The same was true about buying the crack last night, but thankfully, she did not get another OWI. She was back within an hour. By the way, Amy does not have a driver's license; it was suspended because of her last OWI.

Since Amy has been out of jail she has been on the phone almost continually. When I ask her who she is talking to she invariably says, "My daughter," I have spoken to her daughter and she says her mom speaks to her very little. She seldom calls, and when she does, it is a short call. I think she is using her daughter, like she uses other people, to set up drug contacts she can use at a later time. Remember, she is a crack head and a user.

So, now here is what has to happen. Amy has to go. Amy does not want to stop doing crack; she likes it. She is staying in touch with all of her old crack buddies and she made some new contacts while she was in jail. Amy is going to continue to live her crack head lifestyle and use me and my money to maintain it. Amy has no intention of ever changing. She likes the lifestyle I give her and will try to stay with me for as long as she can.

But, all in all, a Leopard does not change its spots and Amy will not change her ways. She was a crack head when I met her; she always has been a crack head and always will be a crack head. It is my opinion that Amy does not have the ability to change, and because of that, she will probably die a death related to crack cocaine. May God have mercy on her soul and protect her. The sad part is that she is dragging other people down with her.

I have gone about as far as I can go with Amy. I have contacted a lawyer and filed for a divorce. It should be final around the middle of August 2011. I wish it were not this way. I wish Amy and I could work this out and stay together, but we can't. We are from two different worlds. The last almost three years have been the most exciting and expensive I have ever had. However, the price is too high to continue on—my money is gone, my health is gone, and Amy is still Amy. I thank you Amy, for the roller coaster ride. It was exhilarating!

Chapter 29

Tell Me Why

After almost three years of research and living with a crack head, this author has made the following conclusions and has the following questions. My main conclusion and question is quite simply, *Why?*

The author has asked many people and has not yet received a satisfactory answer to the question of why people use crack cocaine. The drug is expensive and short lived. The effect only lasts a few minutes before it must be replenished. The cost of replenishment is the same as the initial hit. A seasoned crack user will push (clean the inside of the pipe barrel) after the initial hit. Sometimes this pushing gets them a better effect than the first hit; sometimes it gets them nothing. After smoking, crack users will check any and all areas around them on the off-chance that they may have dropped a small piece of crack. This author has seen crack users smoke all kinds of things thinking it was crack; for example, pieces of drywall, pieces of flooring, including sub-floor, soap, and cheese. Anything that looks like crack cocaine will be put into the pipe and tested.

So, the final conclusion of this is author is still the same: *Why?*

Until someone can answer that question for me, I will maintain my same attitude toward crack cocaine. It is a useless, life threatening drug that should be avoided at all costs.

For the spouse of a person addicted to crack cocaine: I can only wish you luck and condolences. It takes a great deal of understanding to deal with a person who is addicted to crack cocaine. It is not easy to live with that type of person. Most times the relationship will fail.

STAY AWAY FROM CRACK COCAINE!!

Chapter 30

Everything Comes to an End

As with everything that had a beginning, so it must also have a corresponding ending.

This is the ending chapter of this book. I hope you enjoyed the book and gained some knowledge about crack cocaine; I know I sure have.

And so, this is how it ended with Amy.

It was a Friday morning. Amy had to get up early to answer a community service sentence because of a public intoxication charge. I got up with her and made sure she left on time. After Amy left, I got ready for an appointment outside the office and then on to the office. It was starting out to be a pretty good day.

We both completed our required duties about the same time. Amy called me, and we agreed to meet at the house to get cleaned up and then maybe go the American Legion Post to play some pull tabs. As soon as we got into the house, Amy locked herself in the bathroom for what, I thought, was an inordinate amount of time. Finally, I made her come out of the bathroom. Her eyes were dilated, her speech was slurred, and she was paranoid. Amy was high on crack cocaine. Amy knew I was not happy about her doing this. But I knew better than to argue with her when she was high. I waited an appropriate amount of time for her to come down off of the crack, and then I calmly explained how I felt about her smoking crack during the day when we had other plans. I didn't make a big deal out of it I just explained how I felt. I don't think it made much of an impression on Amy.

It was still afternoon. We had nothing else planned, so we went to the American Legion Post to play the pull tabs. While we were playing, I noticed Amy was drinking hard and fast. She was obviously trying to get drunk as fast as possible. That is what crack heads do when they are coming down off the crack and they don't want to. I asked her to slow down, and she just laughed at me and kept drinking. By now she was getting loud, and her language was getting bad. She was embarrassing me. I made up an excuse about going to dinner at the German/American Klub and got her out of the American Legion.

The German/American Klub had their Oktoberfest going on, and Amy said she should change shoes if we were going to be doing any walking. We went to the house.

When we got to the house, I sat in the recliner while I waited for her to change shoes. As usual I fell asleep. I counted my money before I went to sleep, and I had $850. When I woke up, Amy was gone. She had left while I was sleeping. I counted my money again, and I had $350. Amy had taken $500 from me while I was sleeping. I can't believe she did that.

My digital camera was also missing. Amy said she didn't take it. I don't know what happened to it, but it was gone.

I can't keep living like this. I can't keep hiding my valuables because a crack head is in the house. I have asked Amy to find a palace to rent. I know I will probably have to pay her security deposit and first month's rent, but that's okay. I just need her out of here so I can live a normal life again. She will be happier, and so will I.

That's it for this book and also Amy. Thanks for reading my book, and wish me luck in getting my life back.

If you come across a crack head who looks good to you, think twice and reread this book. I have gone through a lot in the last two years, and it may not be over yet.

BE SMART AND RUN!

Chapter 31

Recap

What have we learned from this book? In order to be successful in dealing with a crack head, the following rules must be followed as closely as possible:

- ➢ Don't ever trust a crack head with anything of importance.
- ➢ Don't be afraid to call the police.
- ➢ Be consistent.
- ➢ Don't believe anything a crack head tells you from jail or prison.
- ➢ Never let a crack head have money.
- ➢ Lock up all your valuables when there is a crack head in the house.
- ➢ Don't give a crack head access to any vehicle.
- ➢ Crack heads are liars; don't believe anything they say.
- ➢ Make the crack head accountable for their behavior.
- ➢ Don't depend on a crack head for anything; crack heads are irresponsible.
- ➢ Never give a crack head a present that can be returned for cash.

I'm sure there are other obvious things you should do when dealing with a crack head. Always remember that crack is the most important thing in a crack head's life. Do not get between a crack head and crack—that can be dangerous.

Above all, remember that you cannot change a crack head. Believe me; I know!

Definition of crack head:

1. one who is highly addicted to the euphoria brought on by crack cocaine.
2. one who does stupid things.

Reprinted by permission of Urban Dictionary

Chapter 32

Some People Are Just Not Ready to Be Helped

You have done all the research and found the best rehab centers in the country. You have spoken to the staff at the best one and arranged for the financing. You are ready to kick this habit and start rebuilding your life. There is only one problem: you are not the one addicted to crack cocaine. You are not the one in need of rehab. It's not your decision as to when or where you go for rehab. The crack head is the one who needs the help; she has to make the decision as to when and where she goes. And most importantly, she has to want to go!

Remember Jerry in Chapter 21? He was more than happy to take a break and spend six weeks in a nice warm place with three meals a day. Any ol' crack head can lay off the crack for six weeks in return for plush living conditions, especially in the winter. If the bathroom in his room had a shower and an exhaust fan, Jerry could have had one of his friends bring him some crack so he could smoke it in the bathroom at the rehab center. Remember Jerry was back at the crack within hours after getting out of rehab. Don't waste your money on rehab unless you are sure your loved one really wants it.

Another thing common to most crack heads is self healing. Most crack heads will tell you they can stop whenever they want to, without medical help or rehab. This may be possible for some people, but not many. Crack is a very strong drug. The psychological withdrawal symptoms are strong, and they last for a long time after the last hit. Only one in ten people are successful in quitting crack cocaine by themselves. When the addicted person has made the decision to quit using crack, it is important to support them fully and give them all the help they need. If rehab is not possible, at least suggest the loved one go to AA or NA for support. The twelve-step program is a powerful tool in beating the crack habit. Keep in mind, withdrawal from crack cocaine is more psychological than physical. It may be time to hide the car keys and keep all forms of money away from the crack head. Although their intentions are good, the urge to revisit the crack house may lead them to relapse.

It is also important for the recovering crack head to stay busy. Now is the best time to get a job and start on the road to being a normal person. They must stay away from people, places, and things that make crack cocaine look attractive. That includes family if necessary. Amy has two sisters and a brother, all of whom are active crack users. She will have to limit her contact with these people and never visit them alone.

A good example of what happens when contact is made with old friends happened today. Amy lent her car to a friend, another crack head. When Amy went to pick up her car, this friend was there, and she gave Amy a piece of a rock. Amy drove home and went directly to the bathroom and locked the door. When she came out, she was high. She had smoked crack in the bathroom. This just goes to show you how strong the urge for crack is. All day long Amy was saying how good she felt about having made the decision to quit using crack. Then as soon as the opportunity presented itself, all that talk went right out the window. The bad part of this is that Amy still has urges strong enough to make her use again. The good part is that Amy still has the desire to quit. Tomorrow is a different day, and she can pick up where she left off and try harder next time.

The definition of recovery is: to get back: regain. to regain a normal or usual condition or state.

With effort and perseverance, it is possible for the addicted person to return to a normal life and put this part of their life behind them.

Good luck, and I hope this book has helped you!

Recently, Amy was given a ticket for driving under the influence of alcohol and narcotics (crack). She had to go to court to answer for these charges. The court dropped the narcotics charge and found her guilty on the DUI. They sentenced her to one year probation, loss of driver's license for one year, and $1,000 in fines and court costs. Amy was right back to smoking crack within hours after getting out of court, and she was driving her car. She knows she will have to take a drug screen every time she sees her probation officer. Amy has no fear of the law (see Chapter 15 for proof), and she has been in jail and prison before, so she has no fear of that. The crack is in control. Amy will continue to do her crack without regard for the consequences. Even if she fails the drug screens, she knows she will have to fail three of them before they will do anything. That gives her at least six weeks before they will issue a warrant for her.

This may seem like a pretty poor system, and it probably is, but it is the best that we have. The jails and prisons are overcrowded, and the courts have to be mindful of that. A drug violation is pretty far down on the list when compared to more hardened crimes that require incarceration. So people like Amy will be allowed a pretty long leash before the courts do anything about it. It's a shame because many of these drug abusers will die before anyone will do anything to stop them.

Does Amy need help? Yes, she does. But unless she wants it herself and is willing to actively participate, rehab will just be a waste of time and money. Hopefully, she will decide to get off of the crack and take rehab before it is too late.

It is obvious to me that Amy has passed the point where the crack has done irreparable damage to her brain. When she is not on crack, she is not a happy person. She is depressed and irritable. Apparently she has destroyed the reward center of her brain to the point that it will no longer react without the stimulus of the crack. Only time will tell if her brain will rebuild itself back to normal.

I pray each day that Amy will see the light and make an effort to put this part of her life behind her.

Appendix A

STREET NAMES

CRACK COCAINE

Of the dozens of street terms for crack cocaine in use today, the most common are:

24-7	Crumbs	Hard ball	Raw
Apple jacks	Crunch & munch	Hard rock	Rock(s)
Badrock	Devil drug	Hotcakes	Rock star
Ball	Dice	Ice cubes	Rox/Roxanne
Base	Electric kool-aid	Jelly beans	Scrabble
Beat	Flat bags	Kryptonite	Sleet
Candy	French fries	Nuggets	Snow coke
Chemical	Glo	Paste	Sugar block
Cloud	Gravel	Piece	Topo (Spanish)
Cookies	Grit	Prime time	Tornado
Crack	Hail	Product	Troop

Appendix B

Crack Cocaine

Derived

"Crack" is the street name given to cocaine that has been processed from cocaine hydrochloride to a free base for smoking. The term "crack" refers to the crackling sound heard when the mixture is smoked (heated).

Description

"Crack," or the "rock" form of cocaine, is a ready-to-use freebase. It is sold in small, inexpensive dosage units that are smoked. Once introduced in the mid-1980s, crack abuse spread rapidly throughout America. It is noteworthy that the emergence of crack was accompanied by a dramatic increase in drug abuse problems and drug-related violence.

Use

There is great risk whether cocaine is ingested by inhalation (snorting), injection, or smoking. It appears that compulsive cocaine use may develop even more rapidly if the substance is smoked rather than snorted. Smoking allows extremely high doses of cocaine to reach the brain very quickly and brings an intense and immediate high. The injecting drug user is at risk for transmitting or acquiring HIV infection/AIDS if needles or other injection equipment are shared.

Dangers and Effects

Smoking crack cocaine can produce a particularly aggressive paranoid behavior in users. When addicted individuals stop using cocaine, they often become depressed. Prolonged cocaine snorting can result in ulceration of the mucous membrane of the nose and can damage the nasal septum enough to cause it to collapse. Cocaine-related deaths are often a result of cardiac arrest or seizures followed by respiratory arrest.

Appendix C

Q.) What is the street price of crack?

A.) Typically, cocaine HCl is converted into crack cocaine, or "rock," within the United States by the secondary wholesaler or retailer. Crack cocaine is often packaged in vials, glassine bags, and film canisters. The size of a crack rock can vary, but generally ranges from 1/10 to 1/2 gram. Rocks can sell for as low as $3 to as high as $50, but prices generally range from $10 to $20.

The Street Price of Crack Cocaine

- $40—1/4 gram (larger "rock")
- $10-$25—1/10 gram (smaller "rock")
- Note: Prices vary according to purity, quantity, place of origin and sale, and numerous market trends.

Note: Prices are and have been on a downward trend.

Appendix D

I Married a Crack Head

How to Deal with a Person Who is addicted to Crack Cocaine

Before we begin we must all understand dealing with crack cocaine addicts is not easy. They are under control of one of the most powerful drugs known to man so far. The euphoric high they get from crack cannot be put into words. There is no way to duplicate this feeling in any lab anywhere. Unfortunately for the addict, this feeling is short lived and wanes with usage. The more they use, the lesser the effect. Pretty soon they must binge to maintain the effect.

It is difficult at best to deal with a person who is addicted to crack cocaine. This drug is cunning, baffling, powerful. It controls the mind and the will of the addicted user.

Signs Your Loved One May Be on Crack Cocaine

Cocaine addiction can occur very quickly and be very difficult to break. There are cases reported of addiction after the first use. If you notice any of the following signs, be alerted your loved one may be using crack cocaine.

A person who is addicted to crack cocaine may

- change circles of friends and withdraw from non-using family and friends;
- borrow or steal money to buy the drug;
- compulsively seek crack and dwell on the next use;

- experience personality changes, poor judgment, and loss of interest in previously enjoyable activities; or
- become evasive or lie about activities or whereabouts.

Top 10 Warning Signs of Crack Cocaine Abuse

1. Unexplained mood swings and energy levels
2. Burns or sores on the fingers (from a pipe used to smoke crack cocaine)
3. Declining grades and new peer groups
4. Extreme paranoia
5. Loss of household cash or valuables
6. Weight loss
7. Associating with others known to take drugs
8. Loss of interest in personal appearance
9. Marked agitation and loss of concentration
10. Altered sleep patterns

The user must be the one wanting to get help to stop using crack cocaine. As much as you may want to help your loved one, you cannot make him or her stop; the user must want to do it on his or her own. You can do nothing without the user's willingness.

Keep in mind a person addicted to crack cocaine will lie, cheat, steal, or do anything else necessary to get the money to buy crack. I spoke to one person who was very concerned about his wife turning to prostitution to get the money. I explained to him that he should not worry (other than the disease problems), because his wife was only using one of her assets to get money. There was no emotion involved. It was strictly sex for pay. There was no other involvement.

Remove or lock up anything of value in your home. Anything that can be carried out and pawned or sold will be.

Do not under any circumstances give crack-addicts any money. If they need gas for their automobile, go to the gas station and buy it for them. If they need something from the store, buy it for them. Do not give them money—it will not be used for what it was intended.

Spend time with your loved one. Let them know you are on their side. Don't put them down or ridicule them. Remember, it is the drug that is causing them to act like this. Underneath they are still the same people they used to be.

Always know where your loved one is. If your loved one says he or she is going out, offer to drive. Don't be surprised if he or she disappears on you. Your loved one may be gone for a while, but he or she will almost always return.

Relapse is common, but not necessary, in recovery. If your loved one does relapse, do not holler or make him or her feel like a failure. Help your loved one to get back up and pick up from where he or she left off. Relapse is not the end of the world. The important thing is to get back on track and keep going.

Always remember—it is not your loved one doing this; it is the drug.

Notes

Notes

Notes

About the Author

Raised during the '50s and '60s, the author had little exposure to drugs except alcohol. Then, as a young adult, the author witnessed the onslaught of experimental, mind-altering drugs: first the diet pills to lose weight, then speed to keep you awake, then finally benzos just for fun. In 1991, the author became addicted to Benzedrine and had to be put in intensive rehab to get off of it. This author knows all too well what addiction can do to the mind and soul. Read to see what the next generation of mind-altering drugs is doing to people.

About the Book

What's it like to be married to a drug addict? What should you do if you think your spouse is addicted to crack cocaine? What is crack cocaine? You will find out this and more in this book. It's a true educational overview in a few short pages.

www.ingramcontent.com/pod-product-compliance
Lightning Source LLC
Chambersburg PA
CBHW051422280526
45785CB00003B/1119